The Reference Shelf®

Jobs in America

Edited by David Ramm

Editorial Advisor Lynn M. Messina

The Reference Shelf
Volume 78 • Number 4

The H. W. Wilson Company
2006

The Reference Shelf

The books in this series contain reprints of articles, excerpts from books, addresses on current issues, and studies of social trends in the United States and other countries. There are six separately bound numbers in each volume, all of which are usually published in the same calendar year. Numbers one through five are each devoted to a single subject, providing background information and discussion from various points of view and concluding with a subject index and comprehensive bibliography that lists books, pamphlets, and abstracts of additional articles on the subject. The final number of each volume is a collection of recent speeches, and it contains a cumulative speaker index. Books in the series may be purchased individually or on subscription.

Library of Congress has cataloged this title as follows:

Jobs in America / edited by David Ramm.
    p. cm.—(The reference shelf; v. 78, no. 4)
    Includes bibliographical references and index.
    ISBN 0-8242-1062-X (alk. paper)
    1. Labor market—United States. 2. Manpower policy—United States. 3. Global-
ization—Economic aspects—United States. I. Ramm, David. II. Series.
    HD5724.J6873 2006
    331.10973—dc22

                                        2006017187

Cover: A construction worker works in front of the United States Capitol during construction of the Capitol Visitor Center December 14, 2004, in Washington, D.C. (Photo by Joe Raedle/Getty Images)

Visit H.W. Wilson's Web site: www.hwwilson.com

Printed in the United States of America

Contents

Preface

Jobs matter everywhere. For all but a small slice of the world's active adult population, working is the only way to ensure that food and shelter will be there everyday. But while this holds true for most Americans as well, our relationship to the working world remains distinct, since Americans, more so than people in other countries, define ourselves by what we do. Adults quiz younger people repeatedly on what they want to be when they grow up, and when adults meet as strangers, the first step in a polite conversation is often to find out how the other person makes a living. For people elsewhere, such a topic might be broached only later, since it could be misinterpreted as questioning, for example, the person's social or economic class. But for Americans, professions are the primary stamps of identity. In many social situations, we are shoe store managers or truck drivers or nurse's aides first. Only once that is clear do we acknowledge being Republicans, Methodists, former gymnasts, and experts at making hummus.

The fluid paths many Americans follow over the course of their careers also sets us apart from others. Our educational systems tend to favor general knowledge over specialization—particularly in terms of developing vocational skills—and there is a broad sense among many Americans that education and training matter less than experience or certain generalized qualities, such as communication or leadership skills or simply hard work. Teenagers routinely leave high school knowing only that they have strong skills in some area, such as math, and use their college years to pick and choose from a variety of more specialized studies that others would have been pursuing since their early teens. Even once a person takes a degree as relatively focused as, say, mechanical engineering, few would be surprised if that same person eventually went on to law school and forged a new career as, to imagine only one possibility, an administrator of government contracts for a military machinery company. The combinations are endless, and our awareness of how one path might branch into another has almost made a high-flown political career seem like the logical extension of a successful stint as an actor. All the while, percolating in conversations and perched at the front of many people's thoughts is a sharp awareness of the general wage each profession is likely to command. In that sense, Americans are remarkably serious job consumers. From a very early age we learn to play *The Price Is Right* with our nine-to-five lives.

This book is about some of the many ways that the virtually universal need to work meets our particular fascination with the subject. The first chapter, "American Workers and the Health of the U.S. Economy," considers American employment as a broad political issue, looking at the quantity and quality of jobs available to Americans, offering differing points of view on whether the economic well-being of Americans is improving or declining, and suggesting how American women and minorities are faring in the workplace. The second chapter, "The Role of Governments in the Job Market," considers what governments are or could be doing to ensure that Americans find rewarding employment and enjoy a reasonable standard of living. Two issues addressed in this section are skills training and wage regulation, but the bulk of the chapter takes up the question of how governments can create more jobs—perhaps the single most common concern local and state-level politicians feel called upon to address. The third chapter, "American Jobs and the Global Economy," covers three controversial topics: immigration, outsourcing, and the North American Free Trade Agreement (NAFTA), signed more than a decade ago by the United States, Mexico, and Canada. The fourth chapter, "The Working World in Transition," suggests how changing business practices and shifting social, technological, and demographic factors are remaking the American working experience. Articles in this section provide information on telecommuting, the use of temporary workers, trends among retirees, and the ways technology is being used to screen job applicants and monitor employees. The appendix reproduces a section of the U.S. Department of Labor's 2006–2007 *Occupational Outlook Handbook* and provides detailed and carefully researched suppositions about what professions might be in particularly high demand over roughly the next decade.

The many writers and publishers who granted permission to reprint their work have my sincere appreciation. Thanks are also due to the other people who contributed to this book, particularly my H. W. Wilson Company colleagues Jennifer Curry, Lynn Messina, Mariellen Rich, and Richard Stein.

David Ramm
August 2006

I. American Workers and the Health of the U.S. Economy

Editor's Introduction

In 1992 the political consultant and pundit James Carville shaped Bill Clinton's successful presidential campaign around three themes. The second of these, though often slightly misquoted, has become a motto for politicians of all stripes: "The economy, stupid." For Carville and the voters he hoped to influence, "the economy" meant factors such as inflation, which at 3 percent was quite low that year, as well as unemployment (high for the United States at 7.5 percent in 1992) and the pace of job creation, which during George H. W. Bush's presidency had slowed considerably. Following the election, a widespread sense that American voters had rejected Bush because they were worried about the economy—or more particularly, their jobs—brought home to political leaders across the country that shaping people's perceptions of the economy was crucial to winning elections. After all, most Americans have only a local, anecdotal sense of the national economy. For a wider picture they have to rely on what they hear from people who are or should be experts, and America's political leaders are supposed to fit that bill.

The articles in this chapter take a similarly broad view of the nation's economy but focus primarily on the quality and quantity of employment opportunities available to U.S. residents. To some degree this is a straightforward exercise in drawing attention to statistics, many of them generated by the U.S. Department of Labor. At the same time, assessing the national job scene also requires accepting, as the 1992 election illustrated, that different people have different interpretations of seemingly neutral data—that employment statistics, in other words, are often colored by political spin and are subject to personal bias.

The first article, "Employment Growth in America," by U.S. Federal Reserve Bank of St. Louis economist Christopher H. Wheeler, offers a balanced overview of the American job market and introduces some of the key concepts explored throughout this book. Wheeler distinguishes between what he terms good jobs (those in the top quarter of the Census Bureau's survey of average pay) and bad jobs (those in the bottom quarter) and analyzes some of the demographic factors associated with each. "Developing a young, skilled work force," he concludes, "is probably the most fundamental step one can take in the promotion of good jobs."

In the subsequent piece, Tim Kane, an economic policy expert for the conservative Heritage Foundation, responds to the question posed in his title: "How Good Are the New Jobs?" To Kane, Americans are enjoying a time of exceptional opportunity. Not only are more jobs available, he claims, but these new jobs are generating a broad increase in wages. Kane also adds that fears about outsourcing—the use of workers outside the U.S. to perform tasks that would otherwise be done by those inside it—are misplaced.

In the third article, "As Income Gap Widens, Uncertainty Spreads," Griff Witte for the *Washington Post* offers a picture of the current American employment situation that contrasts sharply with Kane's. While noting some of the same positive trends as Kane, Witte describes a country where bankruptcy, long-term unemployment, and diminishing expectations are rife and where the middle class in particular is increasingly falling behind relative to the country's richest citizens. In "Delusions of Disparity" for the online edition of the conservative *National Review*, J. A. Foster-Bey directly challenges the description of the economy put forward in articles such as Witte's, which, he argues, give a "distorted" view of how middle-class Americans are faring.

Sylvia Allegretto and Jared Bernstein, for the liberal *Economic Policy Institute*, next marshal evidence suggesting that health care costs are eating into the wages of working Americans, offsetting whatever nominal income advances they might be making.

The last two articles look at employment trends among U.S. women and minorities. In "Glass Ceiling? More like Steel," Cheryl Hall argues that, despite decades of active participation in the American business world, women remain underrepresented in leadership positions. As Hall makes clear though, in relaying the comments of one expert, such concerns are "not about altruism. . . . It's about hard-core business results." Edith G. Orenstein then describes various diversity initiatives being implemented throughout American corporations in "The Business Case for Diversity." One executive sums up the importance of maintaining a diverse employee population by explaining that "by having a diverse membership, we bring additional viewpoints and talents to the organization, which are more reflective of the world in which we operate."

Employment Growth in America

By Christopher H. Wheeler
Bridges, Winter 2004–2005

Surveys often find that, among the many issues Americans deem important for the current and future well-being of the country, job growth ranks near the top.[1] Employment, after all, confers enormous benefits to individuals, both economic (e.g., jobs provide an income) and otherwise (e.g., employment gives workers a sense of purpose and satisfaction) and, subsequently, to their communities.

Jobs, however, are heterogeneous in terms of quality. Some offer generous compensation and favorable working conditions, such as flexible hours and pleasant work environments. Others do not. Ideally, we would like to see job growth consist entirely of desirable employment opportunities. However, since that is an unlikely outcome, we would at least like to be able to promote as much good job growth as possible.

What, then, underlies the growth of good jobs? This article attempts to sketch a partial answer to this question by exploring the growth of high- and low-wage jobs across a sample of more than 200 U.S. metropolitan areas between 1980 and 2000.[2]

Types of Jobs

Jobs in this analysis refer to a set of approximately 200 industries identified in the decennial U.S. Census.[3] At the upper end of the pay scale are industries like business management and consulting, paying an average hourly wage of $26.04, computer and data processing ($26.10 per hour) and security-commodity brokerage-investment companies ($26.22 per hour).[4] On the other end of the distribution are jobs primarily in the retail trade and personal service sectors: eating and drinking establishments ($9.95 per hour), gasoline service stations ($10.39 per hour), and laundry and garment services ($10.64 per hour).

In all, the bottom 25 percent of jobs in the sample (roughly, the 50 lowest paying) accounted for approximately 25 percent of total U.S. employment in the year 2000, paying an average hourly wage of $12.04. The top 25 percent of jobs in the sample (the 50 highest paying) also accounted for roughly 25 percent of employment and paid an average of $21.82 per hour.

For the remainder of this article, the former are labeled "bad" jobs, the latter "good" jobs.

The Importance of Good Jobs

When cities create high-paying jobs, there is an obvious gain to the workers who fill them. Yet, the benefits of good jobs also extend to those at the bottom end of the earnings distribution. Analysis of the relationship between the growth of good jobs and bad job wages, for example, reveals that when employment in the good jobs category doubles, it tends to be accompanied by an 85-cent increase in the average hourly wage of the bad jobs category. Therefore, there appears to be some positive spillover effect from good jobs to bad jobs.

The creation of bad jobs, on the other hand, has precisely the opposite effect. As a city's employment in the bad jobs category doubles, estimates suggest that the average hourly wage paid in the bottom 25 percent of jobs decreases by 60 cents. This negative association also applies to wages in the good jobs category. As the number of bad jobs doubles, the average hourly wage in the top quartile declines by $1.05.

> *When cities create high-paying jobs, there is an obvious gain to the workers who fill them.*

Gains in labor earnings are, however, only one benefit from the creation of good jobs. A second is an increase in property values which, given the large fraction of U.S. assets accounted for by real estate, serves to augment personal wealth.[5] Looking at 10-year time periods, a 10 percentage point increase in a metropolitan area's rate of growth for good jobs is accompanied by a $10 increase in its median monthly rent (on residential units) and a $2,800 increase in its median house value.

There may also be a significant benefit in the form of reduced crime. Again, using 10-year growth rates, a 10 percentage point increase in the rate of growth for good jobs is associated with a decrease of nearly one crime per thousand residents.[6] None of these outcomes, however, are significantly correlated with the growth of bad jobs.

Clearly, the growth of good jobs is highly desirable from a number of perspectives. The remainder of this article considers what characteristics of U.S. metropolitan areas are associated with the creation of these types of jobs.

Local Market Size

Overwhelmingly, good jobs in the United States are situated in metropolitan areas. In the year 2000, metropolitan areas accounted for nearly 90 percent of the nation's good jobs, compared with 83 percent of total employment and 81 percent of the country's bad jobs. This fact suggests that the presence of good jobs may depend on the overall size of a local market.

Indeed, estimates show that the growth of good jobs tends to be somewhat faster in more populous cities. As a metropolitan area's population doubles, the rate at which it creates good jobs over the next decade rises by roughly 5 percentage points. Of course, whether or not size itself is the driving mechanism in this relationship is uncertain. A variety of characteristics that are strongly associated with size (e.g., education, big city amenities) may be more important.

Education

One of the fundamental sources of good job growth is an educated labor force. Within the last three decades, the demand for highly educated workers has grown dramatically in the United States. In 1980, the average proportion of workers across all 200 industries with some education at the college level was 32 percent. By 2000, it had risen to 51 percent. In fact, no industry saw its proportion of college-educated workers decrease over this period.

At the same time, it is also true that high-paying jobs tend to have a particularly strong demand for college-educated workers. Among the top 25 percent of jobs in the sample, the average proportion of workers with a bachelor's degree rose from 18 percent in 1980 to 36 percent in 2000.[7] The average proportion of workers with a bachelor's degree in the bottom 25 percent of jobs also increased over this period, although by a much smaller amount: 10.8 percent to 12.9 percent. These results suggest that the growth of good jobs can be expected to occur in cities with highly educated populations.

The evidence strongly supports this conclusion. A 1 percentage point increase in the share of a city's adult population (i.e., at least 25 years of age) with a bachelor's degree is associated with a 1.2 percentage point increase in the rate at which good jobs are created over the next 10 years. Other measures of education yield similar results. Cities with larger numbers of colleges and universities and employment accounted for by institutions of higher education (a measure of the extent of the university community) tend to exhibit a significantly faster growth rate for good jobs.

Education's association with the growth of bad jobs, by contrast, is much weaker. A 1 percentage point increase in the share of a city's population with a bachelor's degree is accompanied by a 0.5 percentage point increase in the rate at which bad jobs are created over the next decade. In addition, the growth of bad jobs is not significantly correlated with the presence of colleges and universities. Therefore, cities with more educated populations tend to see the ratio of good to bad jobs increase over time.

Manufacturing's Legacy

Over the past two decades, manufacturing in the United States has decreased dramatically as a fraction of national employment, falling from 28.3 percent in 1980 to 14.4 percent in 2000. In light of this decline, it is not surprising that many manufacturing-based cities have not fared well in terms of job creation, particularly among high-paying jobs.

Metropolitan areas such as Detroit and Buffalo, each with more than 30 percent of its total employment engaged in manufacturing in 1980, actually experienced declines in good job employment between 1980 and 2000, On the other hand, Washington, D.C.; San Antonio; and Jacksonville, Fla., all of which had initial manufacturing fractions less than 15 percent, experienced an increase in good jobs in excess of 50 percent over the same 20 years.

Although anecdotal, this evidence reflects a pattern that also emerges from a more complete statistical analysis. Estimates indicate that a 5 percentage point rise in manufacturing's presence in a city tends to be accompanied by a 2 percentage point decrease in that city's total employment growth over the next decade.

Why has a strong manufacturing presence dampened subsequent employment growth across U.S. metropolitan areas? Part of the reason may be that workers who are displaced from manufacturing jobs tend to find new jobs (in either the same industry or a different one) at a lower rate than other workers. The Bureau of Labor Statistics has recently reported that, between 2001 and 2003, the re-employment rate for displaced manufacturing workers was 60 percent, compared with an overall mean of 65 percent for all displaced workers.[8] This result may imply that the demand for the types of skills possessed by manufacturing workers has decreased more rapidly than it has for workers employed in other industries. Possibly for this reason, manufacturing's legacy in many of America's cities over the past two decades has been one of slow job growth.

Additional Labor Market Conditions Affecting Jobs

Undoubtedly, a metropolitan area's rate of job growth also depends on how desirable employers find the local labor force. Beyond education and skill concerns, characteristics such as labor costs and unionization rates may influence the perceived profitability of a location and, therefore, the extent to which producers create jobs there.

Statistically, both the unionization rate and the average level of wages across a city's workers have a negative influence on its subsequent rate of growth in total employment and the creation of good jobs. Estimates suggest that a 5 percentage point increase in unionization reduces employment growth over the next 10 years by roughly 3.5 percentage points (3 percentage points for good jobs). Increasing a city's average hourly wage by $1 reduces growth by approximately 1.8 percentage points (1.6 percentage points for good jobs).

The second result, when combined with the fact that wage growth accompanies an increase in good jobs, illustrates an interesting economic mechanism. While metropolitan areas with inexpensive labor may attract greater numbers of good jobs, that growth tends to increase wages over time. This process gradually equalizes average wage levels across different geographic markets, thereby eliminating a city's initial cost advantage over higher wage cities.

Personal Amenities

Where workers are willing to live and, thus, where employers are likely to set up production facilities depends on what amenities (e.g., entertainment, warm weather, education institutions) people desire in a location. Recent research has shown that cities offering a wide variety of consumer goods and services tend to exhibit faster population growth.[9]

In considering what causes good jobs to grow, this study looked at a set of entertainment-related characteristics (numbers of zoos, museums, art galleries, restaurants and bars, movie theaters and live entertainment venues), basic services (numbers of hospitals, elementary and secondary schools), weather (average January and July temperatures), and a measure of how "youthful" a city's population is (fractions of the resident population ages 18 to 24 and 25 to 44).[10]

Of these amenities, only three turn out to be important in a statistical sense for total employment growth: the number of movie theaters, the average temperature during January and the average temperature during July. These last two associations very likely reflect the fact that employment growth in the South and West regions has outpaced that of the Northeast and Midwest in recent decades.

When looking at the growth of the highest-paying 25 percent of jobs, by contrast, many more of these amenities are statistically important. In fact, greater numbers of schools, hospitals and types of entertainment outlets are all associated with a (modestly) higher growth rate of good jobs over the next 10 years. On average, a 10 percent increase in the number of these establishments correlates with a 0.3 to 0.5 percentage point increase in the rate of good job growth.

Good jobs also tend to grow faster in metropolitan areas with younger populations. A 1 percentage point increase in the proportion of residents between the ages of 25 and 44, for instance, is accompanied by a 1.8 percentage point increase in the rate of growth of good jobs in the following decade. While some of this rather large association may be due to a true amenity value of cities with large numbers of young residents (e.g., holders of good jobs may value young, vibrant populations), part of it likely relates to the fact that cities with young populations also tend to be more educated.

Temperature, by contrast, is not as robust a predictor of good job growth as it is for the growth of total employment. Although higher temperatures correlate positively with the growth of high-paying jobs, the associations are weaker than for total employment, and the influence of average July temperature is statistically unimportant.

Conclusions

The benefits of job creation for both workers and their communities are enormous. Because those benefits tend to be even greater as the share of good jobs in total employment increases, identifying where and why good jobs grow is an important task. It is also an extremely difficult one, and this article has outlined only a partial set of results.

Among the potential determinants considered, the most important seem to relate to the characteristics of the local labor force: age, education and (as suggested by manufacturing) work skills. Developing a young, skilled work force is probably the most fundamental step one can take in the promotion of good jobs. Although such a finding is by no means new or surprising, it certainly bears repeating.

Endnotes

1. Results from recent opinion polls are summarized at www.pollingreport.com.

2. As suggested, numerous job characteristics other than pay help to determine its desirability. Many, unfortunately, are difficult to quantify. For this reason, pay is commonly used to measure job quality. Evidence from the General Social Survey of the National Opinion Research Center does indicate, however, that workers tend to view income as among the most important aspects influencing job satisfaction.

3. All job data are derived from 5% Public Use Samples of the decennial U.S. Census at www.ipums.umn.edu.

4. All dollar figures in the article are expressed in year 2000 terms.

5. Robert J. Shiller discusses components of U.S. wealth in *Institutions for Managing Risks to Living Standards*, available at www.nber.org/reporter/spring98/shiller_spring98.html.

6. These data are derived from the FBI's Unified Crime Report. They are reported at the county level in the USA Counties 1998 on CD-ROM and the County and City Data Book 2000, both of which are compiled by the U.S. Bureau of the Census.

7. These figures do not include self-employed workers. Source: County Business Patterns, U.S. Bureau of the Census.

8. Source: U.S. Bureau of Labor Statistics, "Worker Displacement, 2001–03" at www.bls.gov/news.release/disp.nr0.htm.

9. Glaeser, Edward; Jed Kolko; and Albert Saiz. "Consumer City." *Journal of Economic Geography*. Vol. 1, 2001, pp. 27–50.

10. The entertainment outlet and basic service data are derived from County Business Patterns 1980, 1990 and 2000 prepared by the U.S. Bureau of the Census. The temperature data are derived originally from the U.S. National Oceanic and Atmospheric Administration, which is reported in the U.S. Census Bureau's County and City Data Book 2000. Age distribution data are computed from the decennial U.S. Census.

How Good Are the New Jobs?

By Tim Kane, Ph.D.
Backgrounder, June 30, 2004

Economic pessimists have changed their tune. After years of trumpeting a "jobless recovery," the skeptics are admitting that America is in the midst of a jobs boom, with 1.4 million new jobs over nine straight months of payroll growth. Now the pessimists insist that the new jobs are no good.

But if the jobs being created are not any good, what is? Since January 2001, American incomes have risen by 7.5 percent, wages have risen by 2.4 percent, and the government projects 21 million good job opportunities over the 2002–2012 decade.[1]

The charge that low-quality service jobs—often dubbed "McJobs"—are proliferating is inaccurate. The McJobs argument has two primary implications. The first is that wages are declining, and the second is that the new jobs are unfulfilling. Empirical data on American pay, incomes, and quality of life make the case that American jobs are better today and getting better every year.

Yet the real story is not in the spinning political duel over data, but in a much broader understanding of the new economy. Put simply, the modern workplace is empowering individuals to work for themselves, enjoy flexible hours, and pursue dreams rather than survival, all while shattering the traditional definitions of employment.

Highlights

- Average real earnings for "production and nonsupervisory" workers are 2.4 percent higher today than in January 2001.

- The vast majority of U.S. jobs are in service sectors (83.3 percent), and most future growth will be in the health, education, retail, and technology subsectors.

- There will be zero growth in "burger-flipper jobs" relative to the overall labor force, according to U.S. Department of Labor projections for 2002–2012.

		B 1773

☎ Table 1

Improving Pay for American Workers

Change Since		Real Hourly Wage	Real Weekly Wage	Disposable Income per capita	Personal Consumption
Last Year	May 2003	-0.72%	-0.14%	2.80%	3.87%
Recession End	November 2001	0.24%	0.55%	6.92%	8.46%
Recession Start	March 2001	1.61%	1.06%	7.66%	11.17%
Bush Sworn In	January 2001	2.37%	1.51%	7.47%	10.96%
10 Years Ago	May 1994	8.87%	7.03%	25.27%	44.49%

Sources: Calculations from the Haver Analytics DLX database, using data from the U.S. Department of Labor, Bureau of Labor Statistics, and the U.S. Department of Commerce, Bureau of Economic Analysis.

Argument #1: American Pay Is Higher Today Than During the Dot-Com Boom

Multiple indicators show big pay gains in recent years. Real disposable income per capita is 7.5 percent higher than it was in January 2001. Annual real income per capita—a broader measure of quality of life—is up 5.2 percent ($1,819) in the United States over the same period. That is real money, after inflation, that would pay for an extra 900 gallons of gas for every American.

In May, average hourly earnings rose by 0.3 percent, but prices of consumer goods rose by even more, meaning that *real* earnings declined by 0.4 percent. This decline was driven mainly by the spike in gasoline prices, which is already fading.[2]

Real hourly earnings are up by 1.61 percent since March 2001, when the recession began; up 2.37 percent since President George W. Bush was inaugurated; and up 8.87 percent over the past 10 years. One advantage of earnings data is that they count only "production or nonsupervisory jobs," so they are not skewed by rich incomes, but the downside is that they are also limited to traditional payroll jobs since the source is the Current Employment Statistics (CES) survey.

The CES, commonly known as the payroll survey, completely neglects the increasing number of Americans who work for themselves and has also suffered from an illusion of joblessness in 2001–2003 due to declining job turnover. Indeed, the explanatory note accompanying the monthly "Real Earnings" reports notes that many factors "tend to result in weekly earnings averages significantly lower than corresponding numbers" partly caused by "turnover and layoffs." The point is that, regardless of which statistics—even non-inclusive CES figures—one uses, American jobs are higher-paying now than they were during the dot-com boom or, more technically, the pre-recession peak of the first quarter of 2001.

Argument #2: New Jobs Are Quality Jobs

The number of payroll jobs has increased for nine straight months according to the CES, especially in the service-providing sector. In May, service businesses paid 109.3 million—or 83.3 percent—of all 131.2 million paychecks, including millions of doctors, nurses, and teachers. What the payrolls ignore are the extra 7.55 million non-payroll American workers counted in the Census Bureau's monthly household survey. Should these non-payroll workers be considered underpaid or unsatisfied? Probably not. National polls routinely report that one of the most popular aspirations of Americans is to be their own boss.

It would also be an error to imagine that labor data are being interpreted along partisan lines. Thoughtful Democrats and Republicans agree that the emergence of a new workforce is a net positive, while protectionists of both parties dislike change. Daniel Pink, who once worked as Al Gore's speechwriter, is a good example of a thoughtful Democrat. Pink's book *Free Agent Nation* goes into great detail in discussing and celebrating self-employment and microbusinesses.

National polls routinely report that one of the most popular aspirations of Americans is to be their own boss.

Pink argues that several factors, including improvements in information technology, are driving a "broad shift in power from the organization to the individual"[3] in America. Data from the household survey of employment reflect this rapid change, even though the survey's vague definition of "self-employed" suggests that this number may be a significant underestimate.

"Do You Want Fries with That?"

A common joke about the future is that all our kids will be burger-flippers—a joke that plays on misinformed fears that most jobs in the service industry are low-skilled. Services include teachers, artists, athletes, and even cooks. Every economy in history is based on trade and consumption, with merchant retailers who operate the "invisible hand" of commerce. In modern America, they are sales staff in shopping malls, gourmet chefs, and Home Depot shelf stockers.

In 2002, there were almost 3 million "chefs, cooks, and food preparation workers" in the U.S. The spring 2004 *Occupational Outlook Quarterly* anticipates 12 percent growth in food-related work in the decade ahead. The real joke here is that 12 percent is exactly the projected growth rate of the overall labor force as well.[4] That means there will be literally zero growth in "burger-flipper jobs" relative to the overall labor force.

Jobs in what some might call high-quality sectors are a different story. In management fields, the computer and information systems sector experienced the fastest growth (36 percent). The fastest growing professions are software engineers (45 percent); computer scientists and database administrators (42 percent); environmental engineers (38 percent); social and human service assistants (49 percent); postsecondary teachers (38 percent); physician assistants (49 percent); dental hygienists (43 percent); and so forth.

The Future of American Employment

The *Occupational Outlook Quarterly* also indicates that future jobs will be concentrated predominantly in health, education, retail, and computers. Registered nurses earn a median salary of $48,090 and are projected to add an astounding 110,119 gross job openings per year.[5] Furthermore, health care jobs comprise one-half of the 20 occupations that are projected to grow the fastest in the 2002–2012 decade. Computer occupations account for another five.[6]

Critics will assert that America is losing the best positions. However, according to official projections, the top occupations in numerical decline are farmers and ranchers, sewing machine operators, typists, and stock clerks[7]—not IT workers, not scientists, and not the highest-paying professions.

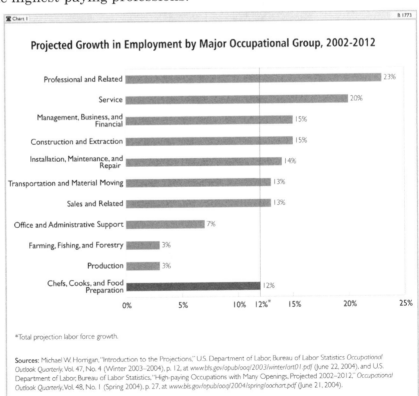

Chart I   B 1773

Projected Growth in Employment by Major Occupational Group, 2002-2012

Occupational Group	Growth
Professional and Related	23%
Service	20%
Management, Business, and Financial	15%
Construction and Extraction	15%
Installation, Maintenance, and Repair	14%
Transportation and Material Moving	13%
Sales and Related	13%
Office and Administrative Support	7%
Farming, Fishing, and Forestry	3%
Production	3%
Chefs, Cooks, and Food Preparation	12%

*Total projection labor force growth.

Sources: Michael W. Horrigan, "Introduction to the Projections," U.S. Department of Labor, Bureau of Labor Statistics *Occupational Outlook Quarterly*, Vol. 47, No. 4 (Winter 2003–2004), p. 12, at *www.bls.gov/opub/ooq/2003/winter/art01.pdf* (June 22, 2004), and U.S. Department of Labor, Bureau of Labor Statistics, "High-paying Occupations with Many Openings, Projected 2002–2012," *Occupational Outlook Quarterly*, Vol. 48, No. 1 (Spring 2004), p. 27, at *www.bls.gov/opub/ooq/2004/spring/oochart.pdf* (June 21, 2004).

Making projections about future employment is inherently uncertain, mainly because the fast pace of technological and social change means that there will be new occupations in 10 years that are simply beyond today's imagination. The Labor Department's best guesses for the fastest-growing occupations are displayed in Chart 1.

Such projections can be misinterpreted in two ways. Rapid growth in low-skill jobs means higher demand and therefore higher pay for the poorest Americans, but it can be interpreted by pessimists as bad news because the current pay for those jobs is below average. Likewise, if high-skill jobs are expected to surge, skeptics will say the poor are being left behind.

However, such pessimism should be considered in light of three basic facts. First, U.S. employment is expected to surge in all sectors and by 21.3 million overall. Thus, far more occupations will be expanding than contracting. Second, the U.S. will experience a demographic shift as the baby boomers retire, inevitably driving up pay for future workers as demand for labor outstrips supply. Third, the future will not be dominated by high-tech brain jobs—a common misperception.

Everyone knows of the financial rewards that favor people with high intelligence, education, and skills. However, in American society, there is a second, deeper trend toward personal, face-to-face employment. Not everyone needs a Ph.D. to do well in the future. Physical therapists, personal tutors, and gardeners are examples of growing occupations that are high-skill but not necessarily high-education. It is easy to imagine an America where all senior citizens are well-cared for, all workers are coached to succeed, and all children are nurtured by personalized educators. Personal attention is a key trend in the future, and therefore in the workforce.

The Outsourcing Ghost Story

The facts on job creation fly in the face of ghost stories about outsourcing America's jobs overseas. So far, the debate over outsourcing has been dominated by a questionable study from Forrester Research, which projects that 3.4 million service jobs will be offshored during 2000–2015. While Senator John Kerry (D-MA) and political pessimists of both parties have repeatedly quoted the study, they do not tell audiences that the lead author of Forrester's study was also a keynote speaker at a Forrester "boot camp" in Dallas on June 22–23 who "walk[ed] participants through all the components of creating and executing on taking IT services offshore."[8]

The Forrester estimates of outsourced jobs are not so much wrong as one-sided. One-sided views of global economics implicitly assume a zero-sum employment market and misleadingly ignore all the gains in efficiency.

An example of outsourcing in terms of *domestic* automobile manufacturing illustrates this flaw. The Forrester perspective is that every new car job that was created in 1920s Detroit meant fewer net jobs in California. However, California did fairly well by specializing in movies, higher education, and *automobile design*.

There are only two definitive studies of outsourcing. The first comes from Global Insight, a mainstream macroeconomic modeling firm, which found that every job offshored led to efficiencies and lower prices that created two more jobs at home. However, the real watershed was a Labor Department survey of layoffs of 50 or more employees, published on June 10. The Labor Department reports that offshoring amounted to a mere 4,633 jobs in the first quarter of 2004, or less than 2 percent of the natural flow of jobs lost.[9]

Conclusion

Congress has a choice: to believe the ghost stories about employment in America, which have always been popular but never come true, or to continue the American tradition of freedom in trade and investment. If Congress arrogates to itself the power to tell American companies how to operate (to save jobs, set wages, and account stock options), then it follows a well-worn path of socialist failure.

Managed capitalism is an oxymoron. Basically, Congress can choose to protect the jobs of the past or prepare Americans for the jobs of the future. It should be an easy choice.

Notes

1. U.S. Department of Labor, Bureau of Labor Statistics, "Tomorrow's Jobs," modified June 2, 2004, p. 2, at *www.bls.gov/oco/pdf/oco2003.pdf* (June 21, 2004).

2. News release, "Real Earnings in May 2004," U.S. Department of Labor, Bureau of Labor Statistics, June 15, 2004, p. 2, Table A, at *www.bls.gov/news.release/pdf/realer.pdf* (June 22, 2004).

3. Daniel H. Pink, *Free Agent Nation: The Future of Working for Yourself* (New York: Warner Business Books, 2002), p. 18.

4. U.S. Department of Labor, "Tomorrow's Jobs," p. 1.

5. U.S. Department of Labor, Bureau of Labor Statistics, "High-Paying Occupations with Many Openings, Projected 2002–12," *Occupational Outlook Quarterly*, Vol. 48, No. 1 (Spring 2004), at *www.bls.gov/opub/ooq/2004/spring/oochart.pdf* (June 21, 2004).

6. U.S. Department of Labor, "Tomorrow's Jobs," p. 5.

7. *Ibid.*, p. 8.

8. Forester Research, "Boot Camp: Taking IT Services Offshore: Getting Governance Right and Leveraging Best Practices," online calendar entry for June 22–23, 2004, at *www.forrester.com/Events/Overview/0,5158,687,00.html* (June 22, 2004).

9. U.S. Department of Labor, Bureau of Labor Statistics, "Extended Mass Layoffs Associated with Domestic and Overseas Relocations, First Quarter 2004," June 10, 2004, at *www.bls.gov/news.release/reloc.nr0.htm* (June 21, 2004).

As Income Gap Widens, Uncertainty Spreads

BY GRIFF WITTE
THE WASHINGTON POST, SEPTEMBER 20, 2004

Scott Clark knows how to plate a circuit board for a submarine. He knows which chemicals, when mixed, will keep a cell phone ringing and which will explode. He knows how to make his little piece of a factory churn hour after hour, day after day.

But right now, as his van hurtles toward the misty silhouette of the Blue Ridge Mountains, the woods rising darkly on either side and Richmond receding behind him, all he needs to know is how to stay awake and avoid the deer.

So he guides his van along the center of the highway, one set of wheels in the right lane and the other in the left. "Gives me a chance if a deer runs in from either direction," he explains. "And at night, this is my road."

It's his road because, at 3:43 a.m. on a Wednesday, no one else wants it. Clark is nearly two hours into a workday that won't end for another 13, delivering interoffice mail around the state for four companies—none of which offers him health care, vacation, a pension or even a promise that today's job will be there tomorrow. His meticulously laid plans to retire by his mid-fifties are dead. At 51, he's left with only a vague hope of getting off the road sometime in the next 20 years.

Until three years ago, Clark lived a fairly typical American life— high school, marriage, house in the suburbs, three kids and steady work at the local circuit-board factory for a quarter-century. Then in 2001 the plant closed, taking his $17-an-hour job with it, and Clark found himself among a segment of workers who have learned the middle of the road is more dangerous than it used to be. If they want to keep their piece of the American dream, they're going to have to improvise.

Figuring out what the future holds for workers in his predicament—and those who are about to be—is key to understanding a historic shift in the U.S. workforce, a shift that has been changing the rules for a crucial part of the middle class.

This transformation is no longer just about factory workers, whose ranks have declined by 5 million in the past 25 years as manufacturing moved to countries with cheaper labor. All kinds of jobs that pay in the middle range—Clark's $17 an hour, or about

$35,000 a year, was smack in the center—are vanishing, including computer-code crunchers, produce managers, call-center operators, travel agents and office clerks.

> *"We don't know what the next big thing will be."*
> —Lori G. Kletzer,
> U.C.–Santa Cruz

The jobs have had one thing in common: For people with a high school diploma and perhaps a bit of college, they can be a ticket to a modest home, health insurance, decent retirement and maybe some savings for the kids' tuition. Such jobs were a big reason America's middle class flourished in the second half of the 20th century.

Now what those jobs share is vulnerability. The people who fill them have become replaceable by machines, workers overseas or temporary employees at home who lack benefits. And when they are replaced, many don't know where to turn.

"We don't know what the next big thing will be. When the manufacturing jobs were going away, we could tell people to look for tech jobs. But now the tech jobs are moving away, too," said Lori G. Kletzer, an economics professor at the University of California at Santa Cruz. "What's the comparative advantage that America retains? We don't have the answer to that. It gives us a very insecure feeling.

The government doesn't specifically track how many jobs like Clark's have gone away. But other statistics more than hint at the scope of the change. For example, there are now about as many temporary, on-call or contract workers in the United States as there are members of labor unions. Another sign: Of the 2.7 million jobs lost during and after the recession in 2001, the vast majority have been restructured out of existence, according to a study by the Federal Reserve Bank of New York.

Each layoff or shutdown has its own immediate cause, but nearly all ultimately can be traced to two powerful forces that reinforce each other: global competition and rapid advances in technology.

Economists and politicians—including the presidential candidates—are locked in a vigorous debate about the job losses. Is this just another rocky stretch of the U.S. economy that, if left alone, will foster new industries generating millions of as-yet-unimagined jobs, as it has during other times of upheaval? Or is the workforce hollowing out permanently, with those in the middle forced to slide down to low-paying jobs without benefits if they can't get the education, credentials and experience to climb up to the high-paying professions?

Over the next several months, *The Washington Post*, in an occasional series of articles, will explore the vast changes facing middle-income workers and the consequences for businesses and society.

Some of the consequences are already evident: The ranks of the uninsured, the bankrupt and the long-term unemployed have all crept up the income scale, proving those problems aren't limited to the poor. Meanwhile, income inequality has grown. In 2001, the top 20 percent of households for the first time raked in more than half of all income, while the share earned by those in the middle was the lowest in nearly 50 years.

Within the middle class, there has been a widening divide between those in its upper reaches whose jobs provide the trappings of the good life, and those in the lower rungs whose economic fortunes are less secure.

The growing income gap corresponds to a long-term restructuring of the workforce that has carved out jobs from the center. In 1969, two categories of jobs—blue-collar and administrative support—together accounted for 56 percent of U.S. workers, according to an analysis by economists Frank Levy of MIT and Richard J. Murnane of Harvard. Thirty years later the share was just 39 percent.

Jobs at the low and high ends have replaced those in the middle—the ranks of janitors and fast-food workers have expanded, but so have those of lawyers and doctors. The problem is, jobs at the low end don't support a middle-class life. And many at the high end require special skills and advanced degrees. "However you define the middle class, it's a lot harder now for high school graduates to be in it," Levy said.

College graduates aren't immune, either. In places like Richmond, the overall health of the economy masks layoffs that have snared not only blue-collar workers like Clark, but also thousands of office workers at companies like credit card giant Capital One Financial Corp. and high-tech retailer Circuit City Stores Inc. Those cutbacks have educated even those with bachelor's degrees in the new ways of a volatile economy.

A University of California at Berkeley study last year found that as many as 14 million jobs are vulnerable to being sent overseas. Many economists, though, say offshoring is more opportunity than threat because it allows companies to make and sell goods for less, and offer even better jobs than those that are lost. "Offshoring can't explain job loss. It can only explain job switch," said David R. Henderson, a Hoover Institution economist.

Henderson says the middle class is thriving, and by many measures, he's right. As a group they're earning more money than they have before, and their ranks have swollen with members who can afford the DVDs, SUVs and MP3s now seen by many families as part of the essential backdrop to modern life. Whereas Census numbers show the median household earned $33,338 in 1967 when adjusted for inflation, that number was up by $10,000 in 2003.

But when compared with those at the top, the middle has lost much ground. And many in the middle have dropped well behind their peers.

The gaps are likely to widen, according to Robert H. Frank, a Cornell economist. He said that as more people worldwide become available to do routine work for less money and as computers take on increasingly complex functions, the demand for those Americans whose skills are easily duplicated could drop. "The new equilibrium," Frank said, "may be a little meaner and more unpleasant than it was before."

In the Washington area, the federal government and its contractors have cushioned the impact of the change in the workforce. But you don't have to travel far for evidence of the shift: Just two hours south on I-95, to Richmond.

From a distance, like many parts of the United States, Richmond looks like a place where the middle class should thrive. As its economy evolved over the past century from agriculture to manufacturing to services and, finally, to technology, it hung on to some aspects of each phase. That diversity keeps the jobless rate below the

---

"I think we're tending not to see any growth in the middle. But I don't know anywhere in America where you are."
—**Michael Pratt, Virginia Commonwealth University**

---

national average. Paychecks for professionals are growing. Major corporations such as Philip Morris USA are adding staff. A biotech park has taken root in downtown. Two new malls recently opened in the suburbs.

And yet, for some who lack the right skills to match employers' demands, Richmond has less to offer than it used to.

"I think we're tending not to see any growth in the middle," said Michael Pratt, a Virginia Commonwealth University economics professor, "but I don't know anywhere in America where you are."

It wasn't always that way.

When Fred Agostino moved to suburban Richmond to head the Henrico County Economic Development Authority in the mid-1980s, employers wanted semi-skilled workers they could train for half a day and hire for life at a decent wage with benefits. Now companies looking to relocate to Richmond just want to know what percentage of the local population has a PhD. "They have to have educated, skilled, world-class people," Agostino said.

Meanwhile, the lifetime jobs were cut short.

The Viasystems Inc. circuit board factory was once known as "Richmond Works," and it provided good pay for people who didn't get past high school—like Scott Clark. He was also among the 2,350 people who lost their jobs in 2001, when the plant shut for good.

Today Clark is a driver-for-hire, willing to work virtually any schedule, and drive any route for less than anyone else. His old factory job was outsourced to workers in China, Canada or Mexico. But now he benefits from outsourcing, doing work that once might have been someone else's full-time job with benefits. A former proud union man, he has become part of the steady exodus from the labor movement, which now represents just under 13 percent of the workforce. Instead, he's part of another nearly 13 percent of the workforce that has grown, not shrunk—those who do jobs that are temporary, contract or on-call.

At least the work's not going anywhere. A real person in America, he reasons, has to drive American roads to get things from one place to another. There's security in that.

Clark used to feel the same security about work at the factory. When he started there in the mid-1970s, it was a new Western Electric plant, part of the Ma Bell family. When managers called him for an interview and he got the job, he could hardly believe it: "I said, 'It's funny you called me. My girlfriend's got college, and you ain't called her.' They said, 'What kind of college?' I said, 'She's taking biology and chemistry and all that stuff.' Before I got home, they called her and I had to turn around and bring her back up."

His girlfriend, Kathy, dropped out of school immediately. They started work the same day in 1976, making less than $10 an hour between them. Marriage followed.

Clark, a big, profane man, makes his way through Virginia yelling at other drivers, yelling at talk radio, and, occasionally, singing along to a sweet, sad bluegrass tune.

He doesn't have much patience for politicians. When Sen. John F. Kerry (Mass.), the Democratic presidential nominee, comes on the radio to talk about the economy, proclaiming, "I believe in building up our great middle class," Clark sneers, "Yeah, right." When President Bush's voice echoes through the cab a little later, Clark dubs him "a liar."

Clark has few nice things to say about corporations, either, but he concedes that the factory—for most of his years there—was run pretty well. He enjoyed the work, putting copper plating on circuit boards that would power phones, computers and even a few submarines for the Navy. Working in the chemical division was a dirty job. But because it was dirty, managers stayed away. Amidst the fumes, working long into the night on the second shift, the workers forged deep friendships. Clark and three buddies played the lottery religiously, with a vow that if one hit the jackpot, they would split the winnings and all retire on the spot.

"It was a real close-knit group of people," said Kathy Clark, who also worked the second shift for years. "We grew up there. We had our families there."

But in 1996, the plant was sold by Lucent Technologies Inc., which had inherited it from AT&T Corp. Although the union made a bid, the victor was a start-up called Viasystems.

Many of the workers, Scott Clark included, had a feeling Viasystems was not invested in the plant for the long term. The reality was hard to ignore: By 2001, few companies still made circuit boards in the United States. They could earn a bigger profit producing them where business costs were lower, and where the workers would not demand overtime or sick leave. Scott Clark was not surprised on the day Viasystems announced the factory would shut down.

"They point-blank told us. . . . 'You could work for nothing and we would still close this plant,'" Kathy Clark said.

On the plant's final day, the workers were told to throw their ID passes and beepers into a box in the auditorium. Scott Clark wouldn't do it. Instead he broke into a meeting of managers, and placed his pass on the table. "When I walked into this plant, they handed me that pass," he told them. "They were proud to give it to me, and I was proud to take it." Now he was giving it back. He turned, and left the plant for the last time.

A handful of employees stayed behind to remove the machines so they could either be shipped overseas or sold for scrap. In the end, Richmond Works was just a shell. The building still sits vacant off the side of Interstate 64 just outside Richmond, a 700,000-square-foot tan tombstone in a weedy field.

Kathy Clark was unemployed for a year after the plant closed. Scott Clark lost time to training as he began his second career on the road. With their savings all but evaporated, the Clarks have spent the past two years starting over.

Working 15-hour days, Scott Clark has been pulling in good money. He won't say exactly how much for fear that competitors will undercut him, but in the Richmond area, he said, a courier can make $800 a week for doing routes less time-consuming than his. That's more than his base pay at the factory, though his new job lacks any benefits and he has to pay for the van and the gas. Kathy Clark, meanwhile, got a full-time job this summer after two years of temp work. But they still have a lot of ground to make up. Had the plant stayed open, they would have been ready for retirement in just a few more years. Now, "I feel like I'm 18 years old again," said Kathy Clark, as she sat in a rocking chair in her living room, strands of light gray overtaking the dark brown of her short hair.

The Clarks know they have it better than many of their friends from the plant. They have frequent, impromptu reunions at Wal-Mart, where the talk inevitably turns to who has found work and who hasn't.

Raffael Toskes Sr. has, but only for $11 an hour. He rides around each day in an armored car, a gun strapped to his side. "I consider myself a middle-class person," said Toskes, who made $17 an hour at the plant. "But right now, I'm probably a lower-middle-class person."

Lawrence Provo has given up on trying to find a job. He was out of work for nearly two years after the plant closed. "That was probably the worst time in the world to become unemployed. Everybody was downsizing. Everybody was laying off," he said.

Provo and his wife cut back on expenses and sold their car, furniture and jewelry. They even sold their home, and moved in with Provo's mother-in-law. But it was not enough. They had come to rely on his factory wage, and now their debts spiraled into the tens of thousands. They declared bankruptcy, joining a record 1.6 million who filed last year.

Provo finally got a job through a temp agency for $8.50 an hour, less than $18,000 a year and a little more than a third of his pay at Viasystems. He was just getting his life back together when, in November last year, his heart failed him. "My doctor told me, 'You've got a choice: You can work or you can live,'" he said.

Robert Boyer retrained in computers after the plant closed. But tech companies told him they wanted five years' experience, not a certificate from a six-month course. So he works for $11.50 an hour at Home Depot, using the wisdom of four decades as plant electrician to help customers pick light bulbs for their remodeled kitchens.

> *"Tech is the backbone of the Richmond economy."*
> —Robert J. Stolle, executive director, Greater Richmond Technology Council

Boyer turns angry at any suggestion that the jobs picture is not that bad. "When these guys get on the boob tube and say there's jobs out there, you just gotta go out there and get them, it makes me want to go out there and grab them by the throat and say, 'Where? Where are the jobs at?'"

Ask Richmond's leaders, and they'll say the jobs are in infotech, biotech, nanotech and other kinds of tech yet to be conceived. "People have the impression that Richmond is a good-old-boy town. And we do have some old money here. But that money is going to build the new economy," said Robert J. Stolle, executive director of the Greater Richmond Technology Council. "Tech is the backbone of the Richmond economy."

One home-grown company seems to capture in its name Richmond's most deeply held ambitions: Circuit City. Born in 1949 to sell television sets to the masses, its existence attests to the enduring strength of the middle class. And all those sales of computers and video games have created a lot of jobs. With a local staff of 3,072, the chain is one of the Richmond area's largest employers.

But the work has a tendency to disappear. In the eight years after he moved to Richmond to take an offer at Circuit City, Chuck Moore lost his job in that company three times, proving that a white collar and a college degree are no protection from the forces that have shifted the ground under blue-collar workers like Clark.

At 35, Moore spent the first nine months of 2004 desperate for a job as he watched his grip on the middle class slipping away. His story complicates the idea that to be comfortable in America today, all you need is a little more education.

Moore's roots are solidly blue-collar: His father worked as an electrician for the same company for 40 years. His stepfather drove a truck. His brother went to work at the Georgia Pacific plant. His mother still manages the local Shoney's. No one in his family had ever graduated from college.

For nine years after his high school graduation, he and his wife, Terry, worked full time to pay for Chuck to complete his degree at the Savannah College of Art and Design. With a knack for electronics and an artistic eye, he wanted to animate movies or video games. "I thought that walking out that door with that degree in my hand, I wouldn't have to look. I would have people coming to me," Moore said.

But while Moore was in school—designing animation by day, manning a hotel desk by night—the technology had continued to improve and so had employers' capacity to hire artists anywhere on earth. A bachelor's degree might have been enough before; now you needed a master's or even a doctorate.

Moore started looking for computer jobs instead. He and Terry both had luck at Circuit City.

Moore's first job disappeared when the company closed a tech support center and began moving its call center operations to India. His second job—designing ads for the recruitment division—evaporated when the tech bubble burst. His last job there ended in January when the database he built to manage marketing projects worked so well that the company no longer needed the help of a human.

Until this past weekend, his job search had gone like this: 320 résumés sent out, six calls back. Three interviews. No offers. At first, he had put his old salary on his résumé: $40,000. Later he switched to, "negotiable."

"I've already been willing to go down 10 [thousand dollars]. And if it goes much longer, I might have to go down 15. For a guy with a bachelor's degree to take $25,000, I might as well be working at McDonald's," Moore said in August. "There's something not right about that."

Yet on Saturday, when an animal hospital offered him work as a veterinary assistant—for half what he had been making in his old job and no benefits—he accepted immediately. He starts today, cleaning out kennels and, he hopes, learning how to use the X-ray machines or work in the lab so he can add to his repertoire of skills.

Moore has thought of going back for his master's degree. But that's hardly an option when he has a 3-year-old son, not to mention a mortgage and student loans.

Instead, to help make ends meet, he's been teaching computer basics at J. Sargeant Reynolds Community College, where his students can identify with their teacher's plight. One is a 20-year Army veteran who found that the best he could do without college was become a salesman at Lowe's, the home-improvement store. He was taking Moore's class so he could go to a four-year college in the fall.

"The job market for people like me is not that good," said the man, Albert DiCicco. "Maybe it is for people with bachelor's degrees."

Lately, DiCicco's predicament has been on the mind of Federal Reserve Chairman Alan Greenspan.

In June, Greenspan warned that a shortage of highly skilled workers and a surplus of those with fewer skills has meant wages for the lower half of the income scale have remained stagnant, while the top quarter of earners sprints away. Greenspan said the skills mismatch "can and must be addressed, because I think that it's creating an increasing concentration of incomes in this country and, for a democratic society, that is not a very desirable thing to allow to happen."

But it already has happened. The gap between the wages of a 30-year-old male high school graduate and a 30-year-old male college graduate was 17 percent as of 1979, according to analysis by Harvard's Murnane and MIT's Levy in their book, "The New Division of Labor." Now it tops 50 percent, with an even larger differential for women. Real wages for both high school graduates and high school dropouts have actually fallen since the 1970s. Meanwhile, wages for college graduates—who make up only about a quarter of the adult population—have soared upward.

The trend seems poised to continue. The list of the 30 jobs the Labor Department predicts will grow the most through 2012 includes high-paying positions such as postsecondary teachers, software engineers and management analysts. But nearly all require a college degree. There are also plenty of jobs that demand no college—including retail sales and security guard—but they pay a low wage.

And yet, as Moore's situation shows, a college diploma offers a porous shield when demand for a certain skill evaporates. College graduates have, in recent years, become an increasingly large percentage of the long-term unemployed. When they find new work, their salary cuts have been especially deep.

The optimists among economists—and there are many—point to trends that could help mitigate the pain of job losses and lead to future growth. One is the coming mass retirement of baby boomers, which could leave plenty of openings for those trying to break into the workforce. Economists tend to believe, too, that trade and technology will ultimately create new efficiencies that produce far more jobs than they destroy and leave everyone, on average, better off.

Scott Clark isn't sure if he will emerge better off. Spending day and night in the cab of a van was not exactly how he planned to live out his fifties and sixties, but he'll get by. He's even managed to save enough money to begin cutting his hours from 15 down to 11.

It's the end of the day now and as Clark battles the Richmond evening rush hour, his thoughts are turning to home. He's already fulfilled his part of the American dream, doing better than his parents did. "Everybody tells me I'm low class," Clark says, chuckling faintly. "But we're middle class. We're definitely middle class."

Yet his kids—his son is 26 and his twin daughters are 21—still live at home because they can't afford places of their own. None of them went to college, although his daughters had 3.8 grade-point averages in high school and his son aced the SATs. They're saving to go back to school—eventually. In the meantime, they work. His son lays carpet and his daughters stock shelves in a warehouse.

Will they be able to move up the economic ladder, just like he did? Clark ponders the question. After a long day, he is showing the strain, getting sleepy with his regular bedtime of 6:30 p.m. fast approaching.

"I really don't know. It's just too uncertain. It really is. There's nothing there," he says, turning completely serious for the first time all day. "There's nothing you can just count on. I wish there was."

Delusions of Disparity

By J. A. Foster-Bey
National Review Online, September 28, 2004

The slower-than-anticipated growth in payroll jobs during the current economic expansion has raised new concerns from many quarters about the rise in income inequality and the disappearance of the nation's middle class. John Kerry's presidential campaign has attempted to use this theme to underscore what Democrats say are the economic failures of the current Bush administration. The mainstream media has joined in, running several stories purporting to document the growth in the income gap and the resulting squeeze of the middle class.

One of the latest entries is an article in the *Washington Post* by Griff Witte, the first in a planned occasional series that will examine the changes facing middle-income workers. Witte's article argues that the middle-class is shrinking and as a result the income gap is widening. He attempts to integrate statistics on the changing labor market and household income with portraits of workers and their families experiencing hardships due to technological changes and global competition. Witte paints a fairly dismal picture of what is happening to the middle class. But the statistical evidence he presents does not support his conclusions, and a careful reading suggests his interviews may be intended merely to illustrate a conclusion he had come to before examining the data.

The article focuses on the decline in median-income households—that is, households with total income between $35,000 and $50,000 annually. Examining data from the U.S. Census Bureau, Witte notes that after controlling for inflation the proportion of such families declined by almost 33 percent from 1967 to 2003.

There are two questions that need to be asked about this claim:

- What happened to all those median-income households? Did they all become poorer?

- Is this decline in median-income households, as defined by Witte, a problem that needs to be addressed?

Let's examine the first question. By interviewing only struggling families, Witte implies that income insecurity and falling wages are now commonplace among the middle class. The reader is encouraged to conclude that the decline in the proportion of median-income households signals that the middle class is shrink-

---

ing, and that the proportion of lower-income households has dramatically increased. The problem is, that conclusion is wrong. In fact, over the period covered in the article, the proportion of households with incomes under $35,000 declined by almost 23 percent, while the percentage of households making over $50,000 increased by over 77 percent. Indeed, the percentage of families earning over $75,000 rose by 218 percent between 1967 and 2003.

This hardly supports the claim that the middle class is being financially squeezed. In fact, since 1967, households have on average gotten richer, not poorer. After controlling for inflation, median household income has risen by almost 30 percent from 1967 to 2003. As a result, most median-income and lower-income households improved their overall income and moved up, not down, in the national income distribution. The struggling families Witte interviews for his article may be the real shrinking class.

While the data does not support the premise that there has been a decline in the absolute economic well being of the middle class, it may represent some other problem. The real point of the *Post* article seems to be that if the proportion of median-income households is declining while the percentage of higher-income households is rising, income inequality must be growing. The result is a bifurcated national income distribution. But there are also several problems with this line of thinking.

First, as indicated above, not only is the proportion of median-income households (earning between $35,000 and $50,000) shrinking, but the percentage of lower-income households (earning less than $35,000) is also falling. In absolute terms, everyone is doing better. The available census data support this: After adjusting for inflation, households in each fifth of the income distribution from the bottom fifth to the top fifth enjoyed wage increases from 24 percent to 75 percent from 1967 to 2003. Witte implies that because higher-income households received larger average wage increases than lower-income households, the income gap has widened. However, it must be noted that on average everyone's standard of living has increased. This hardly supports the assertion that the middle-class is being squeezed.

The second problem with Witte's line of thinking is that it implies we are looking at the same families and households from year to year. In fact, the data that Witte used in his article is not panel data following changes in income for the same household from one year to the next. Instead, it represents a snapshot of all families at a given point in time. Households that fell in the median-income range in 1967 are not likely to be median-income households in 2003. Households move up and down the income distribution from year to year; a low-income household in 1967 might be a very well-to-do household in 2003. In order to understand whether income inequality is worsening it is important to examine whether the rate of income mobility has declined since 1967. If it has become more difficult for American households to move up the income distribution, this may represent a real structural issue. However, there is little if any evidence that income mobility has slowed. Indeed, the data presented in the *Post* article suggests a fairly high level of income mobility.

Given the actual data, Witte's selection of families to illustrate the plight of the middle class is misleading. It would have been fairer and more representative of reality to provide a sample of families that included those whose incomes have improved as well as those who've experienced economic problems. In fact, the right balance would have included a majority of interviews with families who've managed to improve their economic status.

Witte's article is just one in a long line of mainstream-media reports providing an increasingly distorted picture of the U.S. economy. The truth is that despite globalization, technological change, and the challenges associated with recovering from the 2000 recession, the U.S. economy has performed surprisingly well. While there are still some areas of concern, such as the slower-than-expected growth in payroll jobs, the strong growth in GDP over the last year indicates that current economic policies have positioned the U.S. economy to successfully compete. And, if we're lucky, we will continue to see the type of improvement in house-hold income that apparently concerns journalists like Griff Witte.

The Wage Squeeze and Higher Health Care Costs

By Sylvia Allegretto and Jared Bernstein
Economic Policy Institute Issue Brief, January 27, 2006

Despite the fact that 2005 marked the fourth year of an economic expansion characterized by strong productivity growth, the inflation-adjusted wages of most workers' fell last year. The median (or typical) worker's wage fell by 1.3% (Figure A). The decline was even greater for those at the very bottom end of the wage scale, who saw their real wages fall by 1.9%. Only those at the very top of the wage scale had wage growth that outpaced inflation.

Some have stated that the reason for this unsettling result is that increasing health care costs are squeezing wage growth. Allan Hubbard, economic advisor to President Bush, stated in an interview with the *Wall Street Journal* that, "Employers are spending more money on health care, and that's robbing people of wage increases" (January 12, 2006).

The logic of this claim is that dollars that would have gone into wage increases have instead gone to pay the increased cost of employer-provided health care. According to the view espoused by Hubbard and others, workers' total compensation—wages plus benefits—continues to increase at a clip commensurate with the strength of the overall economy, even if their paychecks are admittedly not going as far.

The evidence presented below refutes this claim. First, nearly half (47%) of the workforce do not get health coverage through their job. Second, employers' health care costs rose more slowly in 2005 than any year since 1999, in part because rising costs have led to less coverage (Gould 2005). Third, not only did wage growth slow last year, but overall compensation growth also slowed and by the third quarter, it too lagged inflation. Finally, the growth of corporate profits in recent years has solidly outpaced that of compensation as employers are trading away wage and benefit increases for higher profits.

About half of all workers don't even receive employer-provided coverage

According to the U.S. Bureau of Labor Statistics (BLS), 47% of workers did not participate in employer-provided health care benefit plans in 2005 (see Figure B). Thus, there is no health care

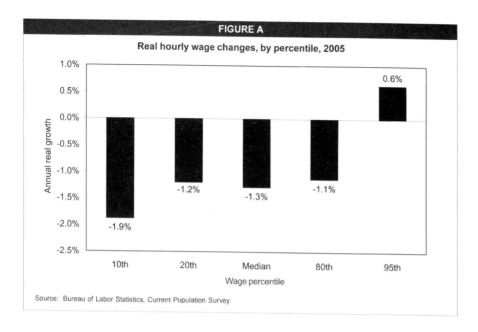

FIGURE A

Real hourly wage changes, by percentile, 2005

Source: Bureau of Labor Statistics, Current Population Survey.

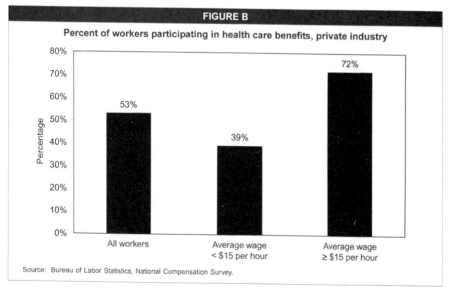

FIGURE B

Percent of workers participating in health care benefits, private industry

Source: Bureau of Labor Statistics, National Compensation Survey.

squeeze that would explain the wage losses of nearly half the workforce. In addition, the BLS data show that among workers whose average wage was less than $15 per hour last year, only 39% participated in employer-provided health plans.[1] As shown in Figure A, low-wage workers also lost the most ground in terms of real wages. Thus, those least likely to get health care experienced the greatest loss in real wages, the opposite of what the trade-off explanation would predict.

Benefits, wages, and compensation all grew more slowly last year

The "health-care-squeezes-wage-growth" scenario has many implications. First, it implies that, while wage growth may lag inflation,
total compensation does not. Second, it suggests that employers'
benefits costs—specifically health care costs—have grown faster in
recent years as wage growth has slowed.

These trends are not reflected in the BLS index of employers'
costs, the most relevant data to explore these relationships (Figure
C). To the contrary, the most recent data show health costs, wages,
and total compensation all growing more slowly than in prior years.

Figure C shows the annual nominal growth rates in employers'
average costs for wages, health insurance, and total compensation,
from 2000q1 through 2005q3. Between 2000 and 2002, employers'
health insurance costs rose quickly, rising from an annual rate of
around 8% to just below 12%. Wage growth decelerated over this
period much as the squeeze scenario would predict, and compensation growth held relatively steady at around 4%.

But since then, the growth rate of benefit costs has fallen steeply,
in part due to declining employer coverage in the face of higher costs
and weaker labor markets (Gould 2005). By 2004, the increase in
total compensation began to slide as well, hitting 3% by 2005q3,
below the 3.8% rate of inflation for that period.

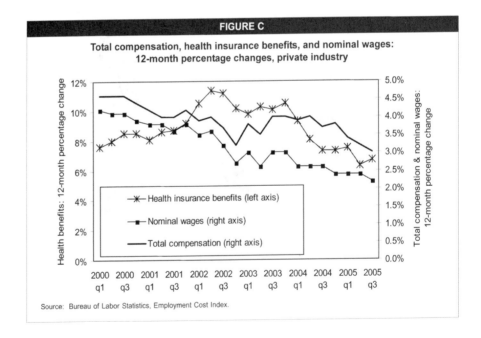

FIGURE C

Total compensation, health insurance benefits, and nominal wages:
12-month percentage changes, private industry

Source: Bureau of Labor Statistics, Employment Cost Index.

Corporate profits unusually strong; compensation unusually weak

While wages have stagnated or fallen behind inflation, corporate profits have remained strong. Compared to previous business cycles, the share of corporate income accruing to compensation is lagging far behind historical trends, while the share going to profits is way ahead of its historical average (Figure D).

There should be no illusion that the slowdown in both wages and total compensation is the result of rising health costs. While compensation gains have slowed, profits have continued to grow strongly. In other words, the recent squeeze on wage growth appears to be coming much more from profits than from health care costs.[2]

The fact that health costs have risen so quickly in recent years surely creates serious economic challenges for American businesses. It does not, however, account for the shrinking real paychecks for many in the workforce. Close to half of the workforce lack employer-provided health care, and those who have lost the most in real wages are the least likely to even have health coverage, the opposite of the trade-off suggested by Hubbard. In addition, over the last few years, as wage growth has declined, growth in health care benefits and total compensation also declined. These trends reflect the fact that strong productivity growth has done little to better the living standards of working families which has been a hallmark of the current economic expansion.

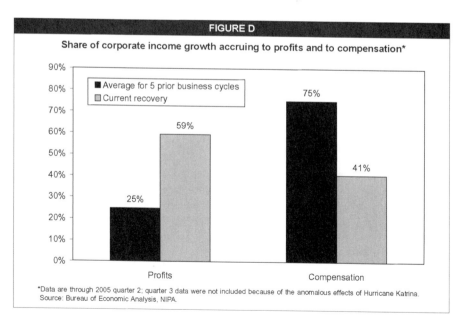

FIGURE D

Share of corporate income growth accruing to profits and to compensation*

■ Average for 5 prior business cycles
□ Current recovery

Profits: 25%, 59%
Compensation: 75%, 41%

*Data are through 2005 quarter 2; quarter 3 data were not included because of the anomalous effects of Hurricane Katrina.
Source: Bureau of Economic Analysis, NIPA.

The authors would like to gratefully acknowledge Isaac Shapiro of the Center on Budget and Policy Priorities and Lee Price, research director at EPI, for their assistance with this Issue Brief. We also thank Allan Blostin of the Bureau of Labor Statistics for provisions of NCS data.

Endnotes

1. BLS data show that approximately 58% of the workforce had an average wage of less than $15 per hour in 2005.
2. From 2001 to 2004, BEA NIPA data show that corporate health insurance costs have risen by 38%, while corporate profits increased by 51%.

References

Gould, Elise. 2005. *Prognosis Worsens for Workers' Health Care.* Economic Policy Institute Briefing Paper #167. Washington, D.C.: EPI.

Glass Ceiling? More Like Steel

By Cheryl Hall
The Dallas Morning News, February 19, 2006

The glass ceiling is a myth.

Surely, that see-through barrier between women and the upper echelons of Corporate America is really made of reinforced Plexiglas.

Otherwise, how do we explain that 22 years after *The Wall Street Journal* introduced this metaphor, there are just eight female chief executives of *Fortune* 500 companies? Yet women hold half of the managerial and professional specialty positions in U.S. business.

Can't you picture the faces planted against the clear, impenetrable surface?

Catalyst, the New York–based nonprofit that works for the advancement of women in business, tracks these numbers.

In the next month or so, it will release its 2005 Census showing how many women have made it to the top of *Fortune* 500 companies as senior executives or board members.

The news will be that there is no news.

"The results are sobering. We are firmly and resolutely in a rut," said Catalyst president Ilene Lang during her visit here last week.

"We had been seeing incremental increases that looked like we might have significant results in our lifetime. Now that's leveling out."

Preliminary data indicate the 2005 head count will look pretty much like Catalyst's study in 2002, when male corporate officers outnumbered females by more than 5-to-1, and the 2003 results for board members, when males held a 6-to-1 advantage.

Why so little progress?

One answer is tokenism: "'One woman on my board is enough,'" Ms. Lang parrots.

Another: Very few opportunities at the top open up.

And there's churn. For nearly every woman who made it to the corner office in the past four years, another faded away or—in the case of Hewlett-Packard's Carly Fiorina—flamed out.

The Differences

One root cause, as Ms. Lang and Catalyst define it, is a persistent and prevailing stereotype that women "take care" and men "take charge."

Men and women both rate men higher at take-charge leadership behaviors—delegating and influencing upwards. Women are perceived as better at caretaking—mentoring, team building and rewarding staff.

Women seek more consensus and spend more time looking for alternatives than men do. Men see a problem and seek a fast and resolute solution. Women think men are going after the quick fix. Men see women as indecisive.

Or at least that's the gender perceptions.

"I don't buy anything that says women are this way or men are that way," says Ms. Lang, who was an executive in the technology industry before becoming president of Catalyst in 2003. "There are many theories and plenty of pop psychology that sell books, make for lots of training programs and [make] consultants rich. But there is no hard, statistically significant data to confirm any of this."

Ms. Lang contends this is trained behavior, not instinctive. "Women are forced into a very narrow range of acceptable behaviors. If you want to succeed in many, many companies, you have to behave like the stereotype. That's what people expect and reward you for. They penalize you for anything that's outside that narrow norm."

> *"All of our research shows that men and women have similar aspirations."*
> —Ilene Lang, Catalyst president

But then when it comes time for the big promotion, women get dinged for not being manlier.

Ms. Lang calls it the "corporate Catch-22."

Rebecca Szelc, who oversees Deloitte & Touche's efforts to retain and promote women in the mid-America region, has her own theory: "Women are promoted on performance. Men are promoted on promise. It's the last acceptable form of discrimination, because it's subtle and covert."

Please don't tell Ms. Lang that women aren't getting that corner office because they have less ambition.

"All of our research shows that men and women have similar aspirations," she says, pointing to Catalyst data indicating that 55 percent of women senior executives want to be CEO, compared to a "statistically equal" 57 percent of male executives.

Nor does she see work/life balance as a female issue. "Men aspire to it as much as women. They may not insist on it or ask for it, but they sure are happy when the women lead the way."

Model for Diversity

None of this is about altruism, says Ms. Lang. It's about hard-core business results.

"It doesn't matter how much capital you deploy or what kinds of investments you make. If you don't have the best people making decisions, running operations and looking out for what's best for the company on a global basis, you're not going to be successful.

"Our economy is filled with very talented women with aspirations. Companies have to create and modify their systems to take advantage of that talent. It's a hallmark of a great company."

Texas Instruments Inc. chairman Tom Engibous has turned this mantra into action.

Forty percent of TI's outside directors and 20 percent of its officers (vice president and up) are women. Its RFID business and two of its largest manufacturing facilities are run by women. A third fabrication manager recently was promoted to manager of worldwide facilities.

And this is in an engineering environment dominated by men.

Yet Mr. Engibous, who has chaired Catalyst for four years, isn't satisfied. He believes the electronics giant's future depends on even greater diversity in leadership and teamwork.

Why does he think his corporate brethren have such difficulty grasping this concept?

"It's not an obvious unwillingness as much as it is a lack of understanding," he says. "Gender stereotypes are real. It's a matter of awareness at all levels, but especially at the top."

No wonder Ms. Lang wishes she could clone this guy.

The Business Case for Diversity

By Edith G. Orenstein
Financial Executive, May 2005

The business case for diversity in the workplace—of race, gender, age, ethnicity and more—has been examined and debated over the years. Despite its promotion by governments and social engineers, the benefits aren't always readily apparent or directly measurable.

Based on interviews with executives at public and private companies and others in the human resources field, Financial Executives Research Foundation (FERF) found the business case for diversity consists of diversity's contribution to one or more of four factors.

The four are: increasing revenue or gross margin; enhancing compliance or reducing litigation risk; enhancing corporate goodwill (to become the "employer of choice);" and as part of tone at the top, when corporate leadership believes diversity is "the right thing to do."

Executives were also found to take a holistic approach to diversity, making it part of their extended role in leading professional and community organizations.

One such executive is Mary Jo Green, senior vice president and treasurer for Sony Corp. of America. When Green began her term as chairman of Financial Executives International (FEI), she identified "enhancing diversity" as one of the organization's priorities for fiscal year 2004–2005. Under her leadership, FEI is working toward this goal on a variety of fronts.

Green explains the rationale behind the diversity initiative, saying that every organization must welcome diversity in order to be successful. "The business world today is made up of a diverse population, and by having a diverse membership, we bring additional viewpoints and talents to the organization, which are more reflective of the world in which we operate," she comments.

As treasurer of a U.S. company—which is a subsidiary of a Japanese company that operates globally and is led by a Welsh-born CEO who maintains U.S. and British citizenship—Green's views about the importance of diversity resonate as being representative of best practices in today's global business environment.

But this concept, better rooted at some companies than others, is still an ongoing process.

"Executives are not always so sure there is a concrete, absolute case for diversity, if they are looking for a quid pro quo from a narrow standpoint," says Johnny Taylor, chairman of the Society for Human Resources Management (SHRM) and president of McGuireWoods HR Strategies LLC, the human resources consulting subsidiary of law firm McGuire Woods LLP.

> *"There are huge opportunities in the ethnic marketplace."*—
> **Renata Pagliaro, Lee Hecht Harrison**

Taylor says in some cases it is easier than others to see why diversity makes good business sense—to tap into certain markets and generate the broadest range of ideas. However, even in the absence of an obvious case, there are other reasons to launch a diversity program.

The four factors highlighted in this article largely reflect Taylor's observations at the helm of SHRM, as well as his experience as an attorney in a variety of corporate settings, including senior legal and HR positions at Blockbuster Entertainment Group/Viacom, Alamo Rent-A-Car Inc. and Paramount Parks Inc. Taylor's firm was recently named by Multicultural Lawyer magazine as one of the Top 100 Law Firms for Diversity, and he notes that the legal profession promotes diversity in part to mirror its clients' initiatives.

Increasing Revenue/Gross Margin

One of the first things a company will try to do in making a business case for any initiative is to assess the impact on the bottom line. A study in 2001 by Roy Adler, Women in the Executive Suite Correlate to High Profits, published by the Glass Ceiling Research Center, found that the 25 Fortune 500 firms with the best record of promoting women to high positions are between 18 and 69 percent more profitable than the median Fortune 500 firms in their industries.

Another 2004 study, published by Catalyst, The Bottom Line: Connecting Corporate Performance and Gender Diversity, found that the group of companies with the highest representation of women on their top management teams experienced better financial performance than the group of companies with the lowest women's representation—including a 35 percent higher return on equity (ROE).

Such statistics will not necessarily convince a company that diversity will boost profits, but there are other compelling reasons to engage in diversity initiatives. SHRM's Taylor notes, "Bottom line, there are times when you design a diversity initiative to implement and supplement your compliance function. It may be purely from an Equal Employment Office (EEO) perspective, such as to reduce the amount of EEO activity in a particular area, or to reduce exposure to the risk of potential litigation." However, he cautions, diversity initiatives must also be thoughtfully planned, so as not to backfire.

Corporate Goodwill: Becoming the Employer of Choice

Lehman Brothers entered into diversity initiatives mainly for talent, says Suzanne Richards, its senior vice president, Diversity. She notes that as a financial services company, Lehman is a firm without a product in terms of the classic consumer definition of the word. "What we have is the quality of our ideas and service, which reflects the quality of our people."

To bring the broadest possible benefit to its clients, Richards says, the firm needs the broadest ideas from a diverse and talented pool. "It's hard to place a price on talent," she adds; but making the workplace more inviting can be one way to help attract and retain talent, to become the "employer of choice." She notes demographics show the world is becoming more diverse, and "we want to make sure we have the best of the best."

"The business case says the world is changing and if we don't change then our competitors will have an advantage over us."
—Ernie Cortez, Ernst & Young partner

Private companies, such as Cargill Inc.—an international provider of food, agricultural and risk management products and services— also see value in diversity initiatives. Cargill's program started "gelling" around 1997 when the leadership team developed a "Statement on Diversity," explains Jody Horner, vice president of Corporate Diversity, and Karen Sachs, a consultant on Cargill's diversity team.

At the time, says Sachs, "we were undergoing organizational changes, and decided diversity would be a key component to fuel growth. The program took on a global nature, setting the stage for how we look at it today: to be very inclusive, and recognize differences exist in people." Cargill's diversity initiatives dovetail with its four key measures for company performance: how engaged its employees are, how satisfied its customers are, how much it has enriched the communities it works in and profitable growth. Horner says, "The link to the business case is the key to ultimate success."

Best Practices

Richards says Lehman conducted a base-case employee satisfaction survey last summer, and has five employee networks in New York—one for women, Hispanics and Asians, as well as employees of African descent and a gay and lesbian network. It also has a women's network in London and three new networks in Tokyo. Each network has a mission statement and subcommittees devoted to employee development (including mentoring), commercialization (reaching out to potential clients) and philanthropy, which is viewed as a way to connect with employees and the community.

Cargill has "employee councils," which Horner describes as being "the eyes and ears at the local level on the ground [since] meaningful actions occur with the input of those closest." For example, its meat-business diversity team has led wide-ranging programs from recruiting to mentoring, offering English as a second language and Spanish for others who work with employees whose first language is Spanish.

On the training front, Richards has found great success using an interactive theatre approach, which has trained 5,000 Lehman employees so far in Tokyo, London and New York, and will be rolled out to other locations. She says the two-hour interactive program "sensitizes employees to the need for an inclusive environment to consider all opinions and the broadest possible thoughts and perspectives."

Cargill also extends its "Valuing Differences" programs through its training programs. "We have tried to integrate diversity training into other training programs, so that if you are going to general leadership training, there is a diversity component all the way from first-level supervisors to senior management," says Horner.

Tone at the Top: "The Right Thing to Do"

Sometimes, executives support diversity programs if for no other reason than that they believe it is the right thing to do. Leslie Jenness, founder of the Scottsdale National Gender Institute—which provides diversity training and support—notes that in working with companies over the past 10 years, the most successful ones were those in which "management was committed to the initiatives, open to finding out from all employees and managers what the major concerns are, and wanted to make the work environment more conducive to each person being able to do their work well and enjoy being there."

Conversely, she adds, "don't say you are going to do something and neglect to follow through, or all you create is distrust."

Lehman's Richards says that support of the diversity initiative is "absolutely unquestioned; it's around us all the time, driven by our president and chief operating officer Joe Gregory." Cargill's Horner notes that CEO Warren Staley actively supports the program, and she reports to both Staley and to Senior Vice President for Human Resources Nancy Siska.

Perhaps James A. Bell, president and CEO and CFO of The Boeing Co., sums it up best: "At Boeing, diversity isn't an afterthought or corollary of our business strategy. Diversity is, in fact, one of our critical business strategies."

II. The Role of Governments in the Job Market

Editor's Introduction

In May 2006 the U.S. Supreme Court handed down its verdict in the case of *DaimlerChrysler v. Cuno*. The lawsuit was initiated by a group of Ohio and Michigan taxpayers who were seeking the right to sue state and local governments and the DaimlerChrysler corporation over a tax break signed in 1998 that saved the company approximately $90 million. The tax abatement in question was one component of a $280 million incentive package that government officials in Ohio had assembled to convince the company to develop a plant in Toledo. The Supreme Court ruled on the technical issue of whether the taxpayers had the standing to sue, deciding that they did not; still at issue is whether the measures themselves violate certain constitutional provisions. To the plaintiffs, the tax break made a rich company richer and personal taxpayers poorer, since they would be the ones forced to make up what the state lost. To the company and governments involved—as well as the 35 other states that offered their support in the case—the incentives used to attract companies such as DaimlerChrysler are an essential tool in building local economies and bringing high-quality jobs to their constituencies. Advocates for such measures argue that while government revenue declines in the short term, the losses are quickly recouped by the revenue the newly created jobs would generate.

Of course tax incentives are just one of the ways governments shape the working lives of Americans. The federal government alone has some 1.8 million people on its payroll, making it the country's largest employer. Moreover, government regulation has a broad impact on the workplace, mandating everything from the number of sinks in a restaurant kitchen to the legal parameters for hiring and firing employees. Yet tax incentives and job creation issues bring into high relief the larger questions of how effective such government involvement might be and whether governments should be involved in private enterprise at all.

The first article in this chapter, "Can Better Skills Meet Better Jobs?" by Steve Savner and Jared Bernstein, addresses the perceived decline in the number of jobs with sufficient pay and advancement opportunities available to those without a college degree. Savner and Bernstein propose a system by which governments would establish training programs to provide workers with more valuable skills and, during periods of economic uncertainty, with jobs that utilize these skills.

In "Minimum Wage or 'Living' Wage?" Elaine McCrate reviews some of the arguments over so-called living wage laws, which seek to ensure that those working full time receive enough pay and benefits to adequately support themselves and their dependents. Noting that these rules are highly localized in scope—typically covering only people who perform services for a single municipality or institution—McCrate goes on to explain how such small-scale efforts are nonetheless having a national impact.

The next two articles address the controversy surrounding tax abatements like those detailed above. As with living wage laws, the use of tax incentive packages is a national issue, though their impact is generally experienced on the local or state level. For that reason, the two selections are relatively narrow in scope, focusing on one state and one city; even so, the scenarios described illuminate the larger national debate. Paul Grimaldi, in "Economic Development 101—The Tax-Break Payoff," examines the methods used in Rhode Island to attract new businesses—and with them, new jobs—while retaining those already there. Weighing the costs of tax incentives in San Antonio, Texas, against the jobs and tax income those incentives ostensibly created, L. A. Lorek, in "Tax Abatements Not Always Good As Gold," finds mixed results.

Governments also stimulate job creation by helping fledgling entrepreneurs. Federally, the most powerful engine driving entrepreneurial growth is the Small Business Administration (SBA). At the agency's core is a program that provides loans to nascent companies. Elizabeth Olson, in "Fears for a Program That Lends Just a Little," details the possible demise of one version of the SBA's loan program, which is specifically geared toward helping new businesses.

In the subsequent article, "The Road to Riches?" Christopher Shea explores one of the most recent and unusual approaches governments have taken to create jobs. Encouraged by business and social policy expert Richard Florida, cities are developing their cultural assets first and trying to parlay them into a sustainable source of business innovation and job growth.

Can Better Skills Meet Better Jobs?

BY STEVE SAVNER AND JARED BERNSTEIN
THE AMERICAN PROSPECT, SEPTEMBER 2004

Our ongoing national debate about poverty, work, and opportunity is in many respects an argument about supply versus demand. Is working poverty ultimately a problem of the skills workers supply or the number and quality of jobs employers create?

The supply-side camp, dominant for many years, argues that the solution to poverty amid prosperity is improving the skills of the disadvantaged. Underlying this formulation for both liberals and conservatives is the belief that our economy—and our society broadly—is more or less a meritocracy. The hard-right position is essentially that the market system ensures that the cream rises, regardless of whatever disadvantages prevail at the starting line. The liberal slant maintains that due to historical inequities, some groups are unable to tap into the meritocracy because they haven't been able to realize their potential. And the solution has variously been dubbed "manpower" development, job training, or, in today's language, workforce development and career advancement.

Then there are the demand-side advocates. In their view, the problem is not the skills of the disadvantaged; it's the number and quality of the jobs available. In the extreme case, demand-siders inveigh against supply-side solutions, arguing that all skill training does is leave its subjects "all dressed up with nowhere to go."

OK, we're being a touch reductionist, but the tensions between these two camps lie behind most, if not all, of our national arguments about work and social policy. Well, now is the time to bury the hatchet and recognize that we need complementary agendas to address needs on both sides.

Let's start with the education and skills part of the story. Expanding education and skills among today's low-wage workers won't change the quality of jobs, nor will it increase the number of good jobs our economy provides. Yet most agree that it is fundamentally important to take on this challenge in order to fulfill broadly shared values about opportunity. Simply put, many low-wage workers need a second chance to gain the education and skills they didn't acquire from our "first-chance" system of public education.

That much is pretty uncontroversial. Unfortunately, federal job-training initiatives—including today's Workforce Investment Act—have been woefully underfunded. While declining resources are a continuing problem, the good news is that a new generation of programs have emerged that dramatically improve quality and reveal the components of an effective system. However, just as these positive developments were occurring during the 1990s, many who were responsible for workforce policy seized upon the weak results of prior education and training programs to argue that pre-employment training for less-skilled job seekers was unnecessary.

Their preferred approach—widely known as "work first"—sacrifices long-term job training in favor of immediate job placement, coaxing people to take any available job from which they will eventually advance. The mantra here is that *any* job is a good job, and that there are no "dead-end" jobs. This shortsighted strategy got a boost in the years after 1996, when Congress overhauled the nation's welfare system and required many single mothers on welfare to join the work force. Well, you couldn't have chosen a better period for this policy thrust. Demand for low-wage labor soared, and the pull of various enhancements (e.g., an expanded Earned Income Tax Credit, a higher minimum wage, and improved—though still inadequate—access to supports like subsidized child care and health-care coverage for kids) combined with the push of the new welfare-to-work mandates to sharply lift the employment rates of poor mothers and other less-skilled workers. Their wages rose as, for the first time in decades, the tight labor market compelled low-wage employers to bid wages up to attract the workers they needed.

> *The mantra here is that any job is a good job, and that there are no "dead-end" jobs.*

Sounds impressive, but in fact some people gained earnings and lost welfare benefits, while others lost benefits and didn't find work. During the late-'90s, low-wage women workers saw their hourly wages rise significantly; they also worked substantially more hours per year. Yet even with more hours at higher wages, by the end of the decade, those at the low end of the wage scale still only had annual earnings of about $9,500. Even after adding the value of the Earned Income Tax Credit, those earnings still didn't get a mom with two kids to the poverty line (more than $14,000 per year at the time)—and no one believes the poverty threshold is a sufficient benchmark for the material needs of working families anyway. Even in the best of times, a work-first strategy did not and cannot alter the economic trajectory of the working poor enough to make a lasting difference in their lives.

What's more, the best of times are behind us, and the employment rates of single mothers fell significantly from 2000 to 2003. The harsh income arithmetic is reinforced by economist Harry Holzer's recent research on income mobility among the working poor. While some people do move up from low-wage jobs, significant upward mobility is not the norm. Holzer's study looked at workers who earned less than $12,000 a year from 1993–95. Following those workers over time revealed that only 27 percent were consistently earning more than $15,000 even six years later. Outcomes were still worse for those with less than a high-school diploma or in poor families.

In response to the evident limitations of work-first policies, there has been a growing emphasis on programs designed to help job seekers prepare for good jobs and advance to careers. This new generation of programs shares several key elements. First, they're grounded in extensive knowledge of the local labor market, focusing on occupations and industries that offer the best opportunities for advancement. Second, they help workers access education and training at community colleges, community-based training programs, and union-sponsored programs that work with employers to design curricula based on the skills that employers actually need. And third, they provide access to remedial services—often referred to as "bridge" programs—so that people who have weak basic skills can prepare for post-secondary-level programs.

There has been a growing emphasis on programs designed to help job seekers prepare for good jobs and advance to careers.

One such model is sponsored by the California Community College (CCC) system for women receiving welfare. When California developed the CalWORKs program to implement the 1996 welfare law, state leaders wisely recognized the value of their community-college system in preparing Californians with limited skills for good jobs. They designed a program in which CCC campuses offer a one-stop shop for students receiving welfare—helping them secure remedial services, child-care assistance, work-study opportunities, and good jobs when the program is completed.

Earnings gains for moms on welfare have been impressive. Prior to enrollment, students had median annual earnings of just $4,000 to $5,000. By the second year after completing the program, women who'd gotten a vocational certificate were typically earning more than $16,000; those who'd completed an associate's degree were making nearly $20,000. While such earnings are still too low by our standards, these gains are off the charts.

Another impressive model is Project QUEST (Quality Employment Through Skills Training) in San Antonio, Texas. Initiated by community organizations in the early '90s to address growing poverty and unemployment by helping low-income residents prepare for good jobs, Project QUEST pursues what has come to be known as a "sector" strategy—targeting industries or occupations that offer good entry-level jobs and significant advancement opportunities. This initiative forged links between the Alamo Community College District and employers in the health-care and business-services sectors to implement rigorous skill-training programs.

Remedial programs were developed for those with weak basic skills to provide a bridge to the community colleges' training programs. And, like many effective programs, QUEST helps participants access critical services like transportation, child care, and housing. The program affects the demand side, too, by working with employers to modify hiring requirements and improve the structure and wage rates for entry-level jobs.

Results have been quite strong, with average hourly wages topping $10 for graduates who have spent an average of 17 months in training activities and broad satisfaction from the local business community. And beyond the individual success stories, the effort has helped promote broader system reform, like improved remedial programs in the community-college system and better collaboration among community colleges and area employers in sectors beyond those targeted by Project QUEST.

A positive theme emerges from these initiatives: Career advancement needs a unified effort by community colleges, community-based organizations working with disadvantaged job seekers, and local unions and employers who can identify areas of future demand and ensure that education and training programs provide the right skills. This is a far more complex approach than work first, and it demands a bigger investment, but it's demonstrably more likely to bear fruit in the form of a significantly improved earnings trajectory. Moreover, these models demonstrate that programs designed to address skill needs can work on *both* sides of the labor market, to meet the needs of workers and employers and, most intriguingly, to have some impact on the quality of the jobs themselves.

Unfortunately, the work-first policies that have dominated both federal thinking and most state and local welfare programs since 1996 have frustrated this whole approach. Instead, we need federal welfare policies to encourage rather than discourage postsecondary education and training, plus expanded child care and student financial aid for adults returning to school. On the job-training side, we also need to move away from work-first thinking and more adequately fund government programs like the Workforce Investment Act.

Now let's talk a little bit about demand. We can't imagine that anyone would disagree with the contention that very tight labor markets are a necessary complement to the initiatives we've discussed so far. We both speak to policy-makers and audiences involved in these issues, and they fondly remember how much easier their jobs were just a few short years ago, how unemployment was headed to 4 percent and employers were importuning job trainers for their best students.

We know that the benefits of full employment accrue disproportionately to the least advantaged and to the lowest wage earners. Between 1995 and 2000, their employment rates grew the most, their wages sharply reversed course, and their incomes grew faster than they had since the last time we hit full employment, 30-plus year ago. Poverty rates for African American and Hispanic families fell more than five times faster than for white families; poverty for families headed by single moms fell six times faster than for married-couple families. For the first time in a generation, median family incomes of minority families grew faster than those of white families, and the gap between black and white incomes was the

> *Everyone who wants to work should have the chance to do so.*

narrowest it's been since we began keeping track in 1947. The workers in these families didn't dramatically increase their skills during these years. It's just that full employment is strong medicine for what ails low-wage workers.

Yet while we know that full employment is the most critical component of a high-wage strategy, it's been the exception over the past 25 years, not the rule. When it comes to increasing skills, we may lack the political strength to move the right policies, but at least we know what we want to do. In a similar vein, we're clear that higher minimum wages and more union power complement effective training programs by improving the distribution of income and the quality of low-wage jobs. But as regards full employment, the dominant view is that it's like beautiful weather: We wish we had more of it, but it's beyond our control.

We don't subscribe to this view. There are policies that would help move us closer to full employment: a lower dollar, more attention to offshoring and job losses related to trade, and, most importantly, stimulative monetary policy from the Federal Reserve. We could exhort the Fed to hang a banner on Constitution Avenue reading "4 Percent Unemployment or Bust," and to keep interest rates low until we return to truly full employment. But Alan Greenspan hasn't been returning our calls. What's worse, even though the unemployment rate is at the same level as when the recovery began two years ago (5.6 percent in June), the Fed has actually started to *raise* rates.

Consequently, we are far from full employment today. In the absence of very tight labor markets, the best job-training programs will simply displace other job seekers, substituting one poor group for another. And even an adequate minimum wage and stronger unions can't do enough in a slack market. What's an enlightened person who appreciates the importance of both supply and demand to do?

Well, here's an idea: when the jobs aren't there, let's create them. We envision a two-tiered system that uses the lessons cited above to develop career paths and expand opportunities for success, raises the wage floor, and levels the playing field for workers and their unions to bargain for better conditions. Second, when labor markets are slack, we create public-service jobs to keep people gainfully employed, drawing on the successful experience of transitional jobs programs that have sprung up around the country using public funds to create work for people struggling to get a foothold in the labor market. Such jobs could meet important community needs and let people use their newly minted skills. What's more, the message is clear and consistent with values we all agree with: Everyone who wants to work should have the chance to do so.

The beauty of this approach is that it takes on both deficits, skills and jobs. Reflecting on the critique from the left, this approach guarantees that recipients of job-training programs are "all dressed up with somewhere to go."

We've yet to work out the mechanics and price of such a system, but it's none too soon to start doing so. In any new system, we need to avoid the errors of the past, chief among them the displacement of incumbent workers. One idea is that the jobs-creation component, likely the big-ticket spending part of the package, could switch on in local labor markets when the unemployment rate got too high—and off when no longer needed. As with any other potentially expensive new social policy, it would make sense to test this idea with a few local demonstration projects.

So supply, meet demand. Our hope is that the two camps can come together and develop what seems to us to be an ambitious but commonsense approach to the stubborn problem of working poverty. Full employment is a great asset, but because we can't count on it, let's create it. Besides, ensuring that all who are willing can realize their intellectual and economic potential is good policy and the right thing to do. Together, they could be a highly potent combination.

Minimum Wage or "Living" Wage?

BY ELAINE MCCRATE
WORLD AND I, OCTOBER 2003

In March 1997, as many as 7,600 workers in Los Angeles got pay raises under the city's new living wage law. Mandatory for companies that got contracts or financial assistance from the city, the Los Angeles ordinance set a minimum wage for covered workers of $7.25, plus health-care benefits of $1.25 per hour for those without private insurance.

The city's living wage has since been raised to $8.32 with benefits and $9.46 without to offset inflation. The beneficiaries have included janitorial, clerical, child-care, and landscaping workers, parking lot attendants, kitchen staff, and dishwashers—workers in rapidly growing occupations that typically pay very little. Syndicated columnist Robert Kuttner has described the living wage campaign as "the most interesting (and underreported) grassroots enterprise to emerge since the civil rights movement."

Responding to religious organizations, labor unions, women's groups, and community organizations, about 90 other cities, counties, and school boards have also implemented some kind of a living wage law for employees of cities, government contractors, or firms that got subsidies or tax breaks from government. For example,

- Three years ago, Tucson, Arizona, enacted a law requiring city contractors to pay a wage of at least $8.26 with benefits ($9.30 without).

- Hartford and Meriden, Connecticut, both require a minimum wage of $9.02 for contractors and businesses receiving financial assistance.

- Gainesville, Florida, mandates a flat minimum wage of $8.56 for city employees only, while Miami Beach sets this minimum wage for contractors and city employees with benefits and requires $9.81 for those without.

- Minneapolis obliges firms receiving financial aid to pay $8.83 per hour.

- Burlington, Vermont, requires $9.90 with benefits, $11.68 without, for city contractors' employees and city workers.

- New York City requires $8.10 with benefits and $9.60 without benefits for city workers and the employees of contractors and subcontractors. Many of these cities also have inflation protection built into their laws (see acorn.org, epionline.org).

Local, Not Federal

There are many other livable wage campaigns under way across the country (including statewide campaigns in Hawaii and Vermont). There is, however, no campaign to introduce living wage measures into federal contracting, reflecting widespread pessimism about the possibility of enacting this kind of policy at the national level. The living wage movement remains a local, grassroots effort, utilizing nationwide networking among activists—for example, through the Association of Community Organizations for Reform Now (ACORN)—and is not dependent on the endorsements of high-profile national politicians for its success.

While local living wage laws require different wage and benefit packages and cover different kinds of employers, they all share one fundamental motivation. In the words of Jen Mathews, director of the Vermont Livable Wage Campaign for the Burlington Peace and Justice Center: "If you work full time, you ought to be able to pay your basic bills without resorting to public assistance." The National Interfaith Committee for Worker Justice, a nationwide, multidenominational faith-based organization, reasons "that as God worked to create the world, our religious traditions value those who do the world's work. We honor our Creator by seeking to assure that laborers, particularly low-wage workers, are able to live decent lives as a product of their labor."

The laws are typically preceded by detailed research on the local cost of living, with numbers on housing, transportation, health care, child care, food, taxes, and other necessities drawn from public data sources. For example, in 1998, a single parent with two children working full time in Los Angeles would have needed $17.68 an hour to pay the bills, and a two-parent, two-job, two-child family would have needed $10.75 per hour per parent. A single, childless person in Omaha, Nebraska, would have needed $7.36/hour in 2002 if he paid for his own health care, and a single parent with two children would have needed $17.69.

In 2000, each parent of a two-parent, two-job, two-child family would have required $10.38 an hour to meet the family's basic needs in Minnesota. A single person in urban Vermont with no children would have needed $10.44/hour in 2001 if he had employer-sponsored health care. A single parent with two children and health care benefits would have needed $19.70. All figures assume full-time work. These numbers are based on no-frills budgets—usually factoring in no money for vacations, paying down debt, retirement savings, children's college educations, or even the occasional fast-food meal. (The Vermont data are exceptional: the legislature wanted to include a slightly more generous food plan and some savings.)

Armed with similar research results from around the country, advocates such as Mathews argue that regular minimum-wage protection for workers is "grossly inadequate." Someone working year-round, full time, for the federal minimum wage ($5.15), makes $10,300 per year, far below the basic-needs budget for virtually all household types in all states. Both the minimum wage and the federal government's official poverty line ($14,494 for a single-parent family of three) drastically underestimate the cost of living for workers at the bottom.

Phenomenon of Falling Wages

Supporters also took a hard look at the long-term picture of economic development in the United States and were greatly disturbed by a pattern of growing wage inequality, with stagnant or falling inflation-adjusted earnings for the bottom 80 percent of men and the bottom 20 percent of women. A worker at the twentieth percentile of the male wage distribution saw his hourly wage fall, in 1999 dollars, from $9.32 to $8.12 between 1979 and 1999—despite the longest economic boom in 25 years in the 1990s. Wages for women at the twentieth percentile of the female wage distribution fell from $6.89 to $6.83.

While wages were falling below basic-needs thresholds for growing numbers of workers, economic policy rarely aimed to improve the quality of jobs.

While wages were falling below basic-needs thresholds for growing numbers of workers, economic policy rarely aimed to improve the quality of jobs. There was plenty of attention to job creation, and there were many local tax breaks to companies that promised to bring new jobs. There was rarely any discussion, however, of what kinds of jobs and what levels of compensation. As a result, supporters said, public economic-development resources were frequently being thrown at companies that paid much less than living wages, with no explicit goals and timetables to improve. Living wage supporters argue that government and companies that make money from government contracts or tax breaks ought to make a living wage the standard for paying their workers, and that living wages ought to be an explicit goal of local economic policy.

Opponents generally understand that $5.15 an hour does not pay the bills, but they invoke the specter of increased unemployment for low-wage workers as a result of living wage ordinances. Mandated living wages will increase employer costs: not just for wages, health insurance, and other benefits but also for payroll taxes. Furthermore, when government mandates wage increases for some workers, companies often raise the wages of similarly paid workers who aren't covered by the law, causing ripple effects. For example, if two employees of a government contractor both earn $7 per hour before a living wage law, but one works on the government contract and one doesn't, the employer will often give raises to both to preserve the wage structure.

Therefore, while some workers will benefit from higher wages, opponents say, others will be laid off. New jobs that had been in the pipeline will not be created. Furthermore, workers who lose their jobs may flood the low-wage labor market not covered by living wage ordinances—employers without city or state contracts or financial assistance—competing for those jobs and driving down wages. While this may not have been apparent in the booming 1990s, it may be an increasing problem as cash-strapped cities and states make hard budgetary decisions.

Living Wages and Job Losses

Economists David Neumark and Scott Adams compared cities with living wage laws and those without to assess the effect on the entire low-wage labor market. Their findings seem to support the idea that workers benefit if they can keep their jobs but that many lose jobs. The economists concluded that about a year after living wage laws go into effect, a statutory living wage 60 percent above the minimum wage raises the average wages of workers in the entire bottom 10 percent of the metropolitan area by 3 percent. At the same time, however, the employment rate of this group drops more sharply. A living wage 60 percent above the minimum wage reduces their employment by about 6 percent. Furthermore, living wage laws might not do a good job of reaching low-income households, since some low-wage workers who are the laws' beneficiaries live in middle-class households.

Low-wage workers may not be the only losers from living wage laws. Since local and state governments could respond to higher costs by reducing their contracting for public goods and services, taxpayers might see fewer parking lot attendants and longer lines to check out of parking garages. There will also be fewer cleaning workers in office buildings and parks, leading to dirtier public places.

Moreover, if fewer companies bid for public contracts, those that remain will have more market power to demand higher prices. If public buildings are still being cleaned, for example, the job will cost more. In short, detractors of living wage laws say they are a bad deal for both low-wage workers and taxpayers.

Living wage supporters respond that the number of low-wage workers on government contracts is far too small to cause wage gains or job loss of the magnitude estimated by Neumark and Adams. For example, economists Robert Pollin, Jeannette Wicks-Lim, and Mark Brenner of the Political Economy Research Institute at the University of Massachusetts calculated that no more than 7,600 workers got a raise as a result of the Los Angeles law, out of about 1.5 million earning less than $10 an hour in the entire metropolitan area. The estimate of 7,600 workers affected is probably overstated because of widespread failure to enforce the law and uncertainty about which employers are actually covered. How can a law that directly affects one out of every 200 workers reduce employment by 6 percent?

Impact on Taxpayers

As for effects on taxpayers, Pollin and Stephanie Luce estimated that under the Los Angeles ordinance, the employers' total costs—including wages, benefits, payroll taxes, and ripple effects—were projected to increase by less than 2 percent. Most living wage advocates expect workers in covered jobs to offset these potential losses to taxpayers in three ways: by requiring less public assistance (for example, food stamps and Medicaid), reducing absenteeism and turnover (which cost governments money), and experiencing greater motivation to do their jobs better (which gets governments more for their money).

Are there alternatives to living wage mandates? Some opponents of living wage laws support the option of a higher earned income tax credit, which is a federal subsidy paid to low-wage workers through the Internal Revenue Service. They argue that it is not likely to destroy jobs, since employers don't bear the cost, and that it is better targeted at low-income families. Living wage supporters usually recognize the importance of the earned income tax credit supplement to low-wage workers in the short run. Nevertheless, supporters such as Jen Kern, director of ACORN's Living Wage Resource Center, explicitly argue that "limited public dollars should not be subsidizing poverty-wage work. Public dollars should be leveraged for the public good—reserved for those private-sector employers who demonstrate a commitment to providing decent, family-supporting jobs in our local communities."

For supporters, the great promise of living wage laws is the ability to increase dramatically the standard of living for a small number of workers, raise the social accountability of companies getting public dollars, and introduce living wages as explicit goals of local economic policy. The disappointment is that more workers cannot be helped with this strategy. Supporters remain confident, however, that living wage laws are at least a small step on the road to livable incomes for all families. For opponents, the promise of much higher wages for a small number of workers is outweighed by the threat of job losses and increased costs for local governments.

Living wages are still relatively new, and information on the policy's various effects is just beginning to come in. Both sides will be monitoring the results carefully in the next several years as low-wage workers and financially stressed cities cope with increasing economic fragility.

Economic Development 101—The Tax-Break Payoff

By Paul Grimaldi
The Providence Journal, June 29, 2004

Economic development for Rhode Island and other states trying to balance their budgets is a race to the bottom line.

In a zero-sum game with 50 competitors, states use any number of incentives to attract new businesses and help established ones expand.

Those incentives can include such cost-cutting measures as low-interest loans, land giveaways, road and infrastructure improvements and tax breaks.

Since the mid-1990s, Rhode Island economic officials have used sales-tax breaks as one way to cement deals with 11 companies they believed would help build the state's job base.

The resulting building projects have created a cable-system operations center in West Warwick, the Providence Place mall, the corporate headquarters of the nation's largest drugstore chain and processing centers for five financial service companies. Also under way is a billion-dollar pharmaceutical plant in West Greenwich.

Ultimately, the state estimates it will give up nearly $27.5 million in sales-tax revenue in return for more than $81.1 million in personal income–tax revenue and more than 10,000 full-time jobs and temporary construction jobs. That would leave a balance of more than $62.6 million in revenues as these tax breaks play out over the remainder of the decade.

"What the incentives do is to reinforce somebody who wants to come to Rhode Island," said Michael McMahon, executive director of the Rhode Island Economic Development Corporation. "We're up against states that don't have sales taxes."

The EDC is contemplating another tax-break request, this one from Tim Hortons, the Canadian coffee shop chain that acquired the Bess Eaton chain in bankruptcy proceedings this year. Hortons is seeking a waiver of the roughly $600,000 in taxes it would pay on the material it needs to revamp Bess Eaton's Rhode Island stores.

The waiver on the state's 7-percent sales tax would produce a relatively modest savings for Oakville, Ontario–based Hortons. In comparison, the developers of the Providence Place mall received $14 million, and Amgen will save $9.3 million as it expands its drug-making facility in West Greenwich.

Such tax breaks go to developments that earn "project status" from the EDC. An agreement with Hortons would be the first time since 2001 that the state agency has granted "project status" designation to a company's development plans.

> *Most states play the incentives game when trying to get companies to expand.*

The term refers to economic development initiatives that the EDC's board decides are important to the state.

Before the designation is granted, EDC staff members analyze the proposed project's impact on the state's finances and the type and pay of the jobs that will come when a business sets up new operations.

The EDC negotiates a contract with the companies that sets a minimum number of jobs that must be added in Rhode Island, a deadline by when that minimum must be reached and sets a cap on the tax break the companies can receive.

The "project-status" program is one part of the effort over the last several years to grow the state's economic base in some logical fashion.

Most states play the incentives game when trying to get companies to expand. Rhode Island has changed the way it plays the game over the last two decades.

In the late 1980s and early 1990s, there were notable examples of individual companies that received inducements to expand into Rhode Island or remain in the state. They included companies such as Cyto Therapeutics, Alpha-Beta and American Power Conversion. Some worked out well, others did not.

By the mid-1990s, the emphasis shifted to tax breaks aimed at specific industries or broader tax changes designed to lower the state's reputation as a costly place to do business.

The thrust has been to develop "performance-based" inducements in which the state provides incentives for companies such as tax credits or financial assistance, but only as the company delivers on its promises—typically jobs.

That approach helped lure mutual-fund giant Fidelity Investments to Rhode Island in 1995—and other financial-services companies—and induced Citizens Financial Group and the former Fleet Financial Group to expand here.

To qualify, companies have to promise the state they will bring at least 100 new jobs to Rhode Island and that the income taxes paid by those new workers will make up for the lost sales taxes within three years.

For instance, Amgen projected it would add a minimum of 250 workers to a base of 150 people. The new employees would include 176 workers at an average salary of $27,000, at least 12 workers with an average salary of $80,000 and 62 workers at various salaries between those two levels.

Three years after that deal was set, work continues on a five-building, $1.5-billion expansion in West Greenwich where the company manufactures Enbrel, a rheumatoid arthritis drug.

Amgen, based in Thousand Oaks, Calif., has hired about 1,150 new workers who are now generating about $960,000 a year in new taxes. Temporary construction jobs at the site have produced about $10.3 million in income taxes. So far, Amgen's expansion has generated about $11.6 million in income tax payments to the state, while the state has given up about $9.3 million in sales taxes on construction materials. [Amgen received another $10 million in tax abatements through laws that apply to all manufacturers, such as spending on pollution-control equipment.] That's put more than $2.2 million in additional money into the state's bank accounts.

About the same time the state was signing a deal with Amgen, it made an agreement with Cox Communications, which was looking to build a regional service center in Southeastern New England.

Cox, based in Atlanta, decided to spend about $9.7 million to build the center in a West Warwick industrial park partly because of the sales-tax break, said a company official. The tax abatement saved Cox about $330,000.

"It was certainly an integral part of our decision process," said Paul Cronin, a vice president and regional manager of Cox Communications/New England.

The tax abatement helped the company secure a property-tax agreement with West Warwick, Cronin said.

In exchange for the tax agreements, Cox promised to add 350 workers to the 972 it already employed in the state. So far, about 215 of those workers have been hired. The company employs nearly 1,200 workers in Rhode Island.

Not every deal saves millions for some companies who take advantage of it.

PFPC Global Services, a subsidiary of Pittsburgh, Pa.,–based PNC Financial Services, opened an 82,000-square-foot processing center in Pawtucket using a sales-tax abatement that saved them about $51,000 on furniture, fixtures and other equipment they bought for the new office. The amount was so small because the company decided to lease space in a converted mill rather than build a new office, said a company spokesman.

But getting a tax break doesn't mean the companies are committed to keeping those new jobs here in perpetuity.

Boston Financial Data Services announced in January that it was pulling its 260 employees out of Providence and moving them to offices in Massachusetts.

Five years earlier, Boston Financial had come to Rhode Island expecting to add up to 500 jobs.

Based in Quincy, Mass., Boston Financial provides record-keeping services to companies and mutual funds, such as tracking dividends, shares and reinvestment information.

The company's Rhode Island payroll topped out at 400.

The pullout exposed a flaw in the state's project-status program, one the agency plans to address as it enters new tax-break deals— the earliest deal did not include penalties if a company doesn't fulfill its hiring requirements.

"Over the course of time, we have built into the agreements a recapture of all of the sales tax," said Robert Stolzman, of Adler Pollock & Sheehan, the lawyer who helps the EDC negotiate the tax agreements.

McMahon, the EDC's executive director, is pushing the agency to go beyond simply getting companies to pay old tax bills.

"Going forward, there will be a 'claw-back' for companies that don't fulfill the agreement," said McMahon.

That penalty could include paying interest on the taxes, plus some sort of fine.

Economists applaud the state for taking that step and for using the project-status incentive as a way to draw jobs to the state. But, they say, a better approach would be for the state to identify which industries it wants to grow in Rhode Island and revamp its tax laws and regulations to meet the needs of companies in those sectors.

Chief among those changes would be weaning the state off reliance on the sales tax.

"Our sales tax is a problem for our competitiveness," said Leonard Lardaro, a professor of economics at the University of Rhode Island. "The first thing that companies that want to come hire do is make sure they get a sales-tax exemption."

Tax Abatements Not Always Good As Gold

By L. A. Lorek
San Antonio Express-News, December 12, 2004

With much fanfare, Golden Aluminum came to San Antonio almost 15 years ago to build a $150 million plant on the Southeast Side, with the promise of creating 200 jobs.

City officials granted Golden Aluminum, and later Alcoa, which bought the plant in 2000, tax abatements worth $1.6 million. The companies also received $5 million more in tax breaks and other incentives from the state, Bexar County and the East Central School District.

In a few weeks, despite the public help, the aluminum plant will close, tossing 175 employees out of work.

The closure illustrates one of the pitfalls when government officials and school district boards hand out tax abatements to lure new jobs to a city. A company gets incentives to open or expand and hire people, but there's no guarantee it or the jobs will stick around over the long term. In some cases, the jobs never materialize.

Yet cities and states are under constant pressure to grant abatements and other tax breaks or they risk missing out on a big trophy. Local elected officials hear from a steady stream of applicants, who'll play one place off another.

While competition for business has intensified, so has the debate about whether the deals are worth it.

In San Antonio, the abatement track record is mixed, and for the first time, the city is asking a company, Alcoa, for some money back.

"Some of these things have gone away—yes—but it's not because we as a community have made a mistake in granting these things," said Mario Hernandez, president of the San Antonio Economic Development Foundation. "They have gone away because of market factors."

Since 1989, the city has granted companies 57 tax abatements, giving up $22.5 million in revenue, according to *San Antonio Express-News* research. The businesses promised 17,012 full-time jobs when they announced their projects, and so far have delivered 17,131 that still exist, the *Express-News* found.

In addition to the city tax abatements, many of the companies received tax breaks from the county and some school districts. Other incentives can include state job training funds, grants and access to capital, lower-cost land, sales tax rebates, enterprise development zones, tax increment financing and more.

City officials say tax abatements have played a big role in San Antonio's growth by helping to attract a total investment of $1.3 billion, according to Ramiro Cavazos, director of the city's economic development department.

He said the projects have generated $52.7 million in taxes, not including sales tax and public utility revenues.

San Antonio has attracted some great jobs because of abatements, which have allowed the city to compete for projects that otherwise might not have even considered it, Hernandez said.

For example, World Savings Bank invested $46 million to build a four-building campus in San Antonio. It received a 10-year tax abatement worth $2 million from the city and a similar abatement from the county.

The company has created 2,261 jobs in the financial services industry that still are here and now has a nine-building campus. Golden West Financial Corp., its parent company, also is rumored to be looking at San Antonio to add 2,000 more jobs.

"For the very small investment this community made, that is a phenomenal story," Hernandez said.

Another success is Boeing Aerospace Operations, which received a $1.03 million tax break from the city in 1999 on its aircraft repair facility at KellyUSA. Boeing promised to hire 2,000 employees at the former Kelly AFB, which closed in 2001, and today it has a work force of 2,513.

But 42 percent of the city tax abatements were granted to companies that shut down, transferred their abatement to another company or didn't follow through on the approved project after all, the Express-News found.

Besides Golden Aluminum/Alcoa, other tax abatement recipients that have closed include discount retailer Solo Serve, sunglasses manufacturer Bausch & Lomb, Sony Microelectronics' chip manufacturing plant, AMR Information Services' call center for American Airlines and Amnitek, a computer parts manufacturer.

Alcoa's shutdown prompted the city to seek a tax rebate of $500,000 from the company, said Ramiro Cavazos, director of the city's economic development department.

The city is relying on a "claw-back" agreement, a legally binding clause in the tax abatement contract that allows it to go after companies that don't live up to their promises.

Nationwide, the use of tax abatement and tax increment financing or TIFs have been on the rise as economic development tools to draw new business, said Bernard L. Weinstein, director of the Center for Economic Development and Research at the University of North Texas in Denton.

All 50 states offer either abatements or tax increment financing for projects.

"Tax abatements are a fact of life," said Carlton Schwab, president of the Texas Economic Development Council in Austin. "It is critically important for us to be able to do it, because our property taxes are so high."

Yet abatements do come with a cost. When a company receives one, government officials decide to exempt all or some of its property, such as land, buildings, inventory, machinery or other equipment, from taxes for a set number of years. Abatements lower taxes for the companies, but the city gives up some of its tax base.

"We have a long history of not making enormously wise and thoughtful strategic decisions when it comes to economic development," said Heywood Sanders, professor of public policy at the University of Texas at San Antonio.

Abatements Add Up

The city's largest tax abatement, originally estimated to be worth $7.5 million, went in 1989 to Sea World, which also received abatements from the county and Northside School District. City officials at first said they wouldn't annex the theme park's land for 15 years, but when they did annex the land in 1993, Sea World was given a tax abatement to help make up for the annexation.

The original developers promised 1,500 full-time jobs for a year-round attraction, but today the park, under new ownership, has 250 full-time employees and operates primarily in the summer with another 2,500 seasonal workers.

Among the city's 10 largest tax abatements, officials granted only two to manufacturers: $1.6 million to Golden Aluminum and an estimated $2.3 million to Dee Howard, which now belongs to S.A. Aerospace. Two went to financial services operations centers: $2.7 million to World Savings Bank and nearly $6 million in four different tax abatement agreements to Chase Bank Credit Card Services.

San Antonio's thriving tourism and hospitality industry garnered a huge chunk of abatements, with four going to hotels including $2.7 million for the Westin La Cantera Resort Hotel, $2.4 million for the Hyatt Resort, $2.1 million for the Adam's Mark Hotel (now Crowne Plaza) and $2.1 million to the Westin Riverwalk Hotel.

City officials also approved abatements for projects that never were done, including the proposed $60 million Greystone Resort Hotel and golf course on the Northwest Side and a $200 million ITT Sheraton convention center hotel downtown.

In some cases, city officials approved tax abatements that lasted longer than the companies, and the jobs promised never materialized or vanished after a few years. Colin Medical Instruments Corp., which received a six-year tax abatement on its $2.5 million North Side plant and pledged to create 500 jobs, has 35 employees today.

While tax abatements can help create jobs, many of the ones San Antonio granted resulted in the creation of lower-wage jobs at call centers, hotels and theme parks, UTSA's Sanders said.

In addition, some of the tax abatements have gone to multibillion-dollar companies that already existed in San Antonio, such as H.E. Butt Grocery Co., H.B. Zachry and Valero Energy. Other local companies to receive tax abatements include Alamo Iron Works, Richter's Bakery, Frito-Lay, Oberthur Gaming Technologies, and DPT Laboratories.

San Antonio–based USAA's subsidiary, La Cantera Development Co., received a $4.7 million, 10-year tax abatement to build Fiesta Texas and a $2.7 million tax abatement to build Westin La Cantera Resort Hotel.

Economic development officials contend that existing companies also need tax abatements to expand locally or they might get lured to another city. H.B. Zachry, a home-grown construction giant, threatened to move its headquarters to Schertz, just outside the city.

Cutting taxes or offering abatements . . .
[is] "one of the futile things that cities try to
do to grow their economic base."
—Rachel Weber, University of Illinois at Chicago

The trouble with tax abatements is that a lot of companies that get them don't need help, Weinstein said. "Those people would have come anyway."

Cutting taxes or offering abatements doesn't automatically lead to net job growth or enhanced property values, said Rachel Weber, associate professor of urban planning with the University of Illinois at Chicago. "It's one of the futile things that cities try to do to grow their economic base," Weber said.

Better Accountability

In response to some of the failures, San Antonio officials have tightened up the tax abatement program to make companies more accountable for the jobs and investment they promise.

In 1998, the activist groups Communities Organized for Public Service (COPS) and the Metropolitan Alliance persuaded the City Council to require companies with tax abatements to pay a "living wage."

Today, companies receiving tax abatements from the city must pay workers between $8.85 and $10.94 an hour, plus benefits such as health insurance and retirement plans.

"What we expect out of the tax abatements is jobs," said Tim McCallum, the spokesman for COPS–Metro Alliance and an accountant. "We don't want to invest in minimum-wage jobs. We've got plenty of them."

In addition, the city's tax abatements now contain beefy "claw-back" agreements that require companies to pay back taxes if they don't produce the investment and jobs promised. That claw-back clause is allowing the city to go after Alcoa for taxes.

"Before they had these claw-back agreements, there were no requirements," McCallum said. Companies would sign the agreements and not live up to the promises and just walk away tax free, he said.

City officials now restrict the length of the abatement and tie it directly to job creation. A company can receive an abatement up to a maximum of 10 years. The earlier abatements, such as the one granted to Golden Aluminum, stretched on for 15 years.

The city also restricts where a company can locate. This year, it banned tax abatements to companies building over the Edwards Aquifer recharge zone, the watershed for the city's water supply. It also doesn't grant abatements to call centers and most hotel projects or retail stores.

City Council members turned down a tax abatement earlier this year for a Target store on the Southeast Side, but the retailer set up shop anyway.

During the past 15 years, San Antonio leaders have seen some good come out of the failures. Sony left San Antonio last year, but it contributed to building the city's Japan relationship, which helped lay the foundation to attract Toyota, which will open an $800 million plant here, Cavazos said.

In 1994, the city approved a tax abatement for Sony worth $1.1 million for six years. Sony pledged to spend $260 million to upgrade its equipment at the plant and create 100 to 150 new jobs. At the end of the expansion, the plant was expected to employ 1,000 people, but it never reached that level.

When Sony shut down last year, the company had 600 employees. Sony's tax abatement helped prolong the life of the plant, which Hernandez called a smart move, because it preserved some good-paying jobs a little longer.

But Amnitek, which received a 10-year tax abatement in 1999, never used more than 10 percent of its 92,000-square-foot building before it shut down.

The Economic Development Foundation has tried to recruit companies to the site, but it's a highly specialized building meant for stamping and injection molding.

Another failure, American Airlines, received an abatement beginning in 1991 to build a $11 million call center that created nearly 1,500 jobs but it shut down in 2001 at the end of its 10-year term.

The county successfully went after the airline for abated taxes. The city couldn't, because it did not have a clawback agreement with the company.

When deciding where to locate a project today, companies often look for an educated work force, low utility costs, an attractive quality of life, good infrastructure and education. Tax abatements provide an extra incentive. "In times of fiscal austerity, you can't go spending all of your money on tax abatements," Weber said.

Abatements are important, Cavazos said, but they aren't the only means of attracting companies. In fact, 127 companies have moved to San Antonio since 1991 and only 21 of those, or 16 percent, used the city's tax abatement program, he said.

Economic incentives don't break deals, said Hernandez, with the San Antonio Economic Development Foundation.

"It's proximity to market. Proximity to the best-prepared labor force."

To illustrate the point, San Antonio and Texas offered the lowest incentive package out of all the states vying for Toyota's truck plant with 2,000 jobs, but it still landed the project.

San Antonio offered $133.2 million in direct benefits to attract Toyota, while rivals in Tennessee, Alabama and Mississippi offered deals ranging from $150 million to $500 million.

When it comes to incentives, a city doesn't have to be the biggest, Hernandez said. "You don't want to go out and buy companies." But as Golden Aluminum and Alcoa illustrate, economic development officials want the jobs and company to last longer than the tax abatement.

Fears for a Program That Lends Just a Little

By Elizabeth Olson
The New York Times, March 17, 2005

Since the beginning of the 1990's, thousands of aspiring entrepreneurs have moved away from unemployment or welfare by borrowing a few thousand dollars—even as little as $500—to set up their own small business.

Diane Holloway, a single mother and out-of-work pastry chef, used a $5,000 loan from a local women's economic agency in Silver City, N.M., several years ago to cobble together a restaurant in an old storefront, cooking for customers with a scavenged pizza oven and serving them on a half-dozen mismatched tables.

"That money made the difference," said Mrs. Holloway, whose restaurant, Diane's, is now thriving, with 30 employees. She plans to open two more restaurants next year. "Without it, I wouldn't have had a chance to get my business going."

Now the modest financial backing that Mrs. Holloway and other women and minorities have used to create jobs for themselves and others may soon be shut off. The Bush administration has proposed ending the funding for the Small Business Administration's microloan program, which provides seed money and technical assistance to start-ups and low-income entrepreneurs.

Small-business owners like Mrs. Holloway were wooed in the recent election by both parties, which hailed them as driving the American economy by creating millions of jobs across the country. But now that budget time is here, a political debate is boiling over administration proposals to scale back small-business programs.

Two of the S.B.A.'s signature loan programs are in trouble, according to some members of Congress who support them.

One, the microloan program, is targeted for elimination. It lent almost $33 million to 2,400 entrepreneurs in fiscal 2004, and is one of 10 agency programs set for termination in the budget proposed by President Bush for 2006. Supporters argue that a microloan is almost always the essential first step to success for women and minorities, who usually do not have the money, credit history or collateral to borrow from a commercial bank.

The other, the S.B.A.'s giant 7 (a) guaranteed loan program, is in turmoil. While it is not expected to be cut back, it has been operating on fees generated by its loans after running out of money in

2004. Supporters fear it may eventually be slated for elimination, following the pattern of another loan program, intended to help high-technology companies, that the administration now proposes ending.

The guaranteed loan program backed $12.7 billion in loans in fiscal 2004 to nearly 75,000 businesses.

Women have received the greatest share of microloans.

Defenders of the administration's proposed cutbacks, including the agency's administrator, Hector V. Barreto, say that, in reality, money for small businesses will be little affected, and the government will save by not having to pay for the technical assistance that the law requires for loan recipients.

There is little chance that Congress, which has resisted previous administration efforts to prune the agency's budget heavily, will approve the proposed Bush administration cutbacks wholesale. Some influential Republicans are opposed, including Senator Olympia J. Snowe of Maine, the chairwoman of the Committee on Small Business and Entrepreneurship. Still, advocates of the program say the proposals are a serious threat to a program that has an exemplary record of success.

Women have received the greatest share of microloans, where the S.B.A. furnishes seed capital for lending by intermediaries, usually local nonprofit groups. According to Congressional data for fiscal 2004, more than 60 percent of such loans went to women, and the program had a default rate of just over 1 percent. The government also spent $15 million on technical assistance.

Teri Wade, who used a $5,000 microloan to open a salon in Herndon, Va., offering cellulite-reduction treatments, said that the hands-on assistance she received was crucial to her start-up.

"I would have made major mistakes," she said, "like not getting liability insurance, or giving away too much of my business to get financing. Without that advice, I wouldn't be in business."

The S.B.A. maintains that microloans, which average $13,600, can be folded into its guaranteed loan program, where the average loan is $15,300. The agency said that around one-third of guaranteed loans were under $35,000, indicating that they were borrowings by start-up firms.

The members of Congress said that recent changes in the way the guaranteed loan program was run, especially higher fees for borrowers and lenders, have already crimped the ability of small businesses to get loans. Moreover, they say, the fees and paperwork make smaller loans uneconomical for many banks.

Last October, the S.B.A.'s guaranteed loan program was shifted to fee-only, meaning the program receives its support from fees charged to borrowers and banks, and does not have yearly Congressional appropriations to make up any financial shortfall. As a result, the fees have risen, to as much as double on some loans.

"The borrower's costs are now double for the smaller loans of up to $150,000," said Richard Proudfit, chief executive of the Gateway Business Bank, a small bank in Cerritos, Calif., that lends to small businesses.

Mr. Barreto, the S.B.A. administrator, said higher fees had not curbed credit, citing statistics that S.B.A.–backed lending rose 11 percent in the last quarter of 2004 from a year earlier, to $4.4 billion.

But Representative Nydia Velazquez of New York, the senior Democrat on the House Small Business Committee, argued that higher fees were pushing lenders out of the picture. For example, she said that in 2001, more than 5,000 banks made S.B.A.–backed loans; three years later, only half as many banks did so. And she contested Mr. Barreto's claim of increased S.B.A. lending, saying that the agency's lending declined by about 10 percent in the last quarter of 2004, to $3.56 billion.

"It's fine and dandy to be talking about 7(a) loans, but those are not for start-ups, they are for established businesses."
—Teri Wade, salon owner, Herndon, Va.

The members of Congress say that confidence in the agency's guaranteed loan program has been undermined, citing the disruption caused when the program ran out of money in early 2004 and was shut down for two weeks until an emergency appropriation was made. Then last April, the maximum amount of money businesses could borrow was lowered temporarily to $750,000, from $1.5 million.

That was damaging to some ventures. Marilyn Landis, a consultant for small businesses, said that lack of funding sank the effort of an established Pittsburgh trucking company to expand by buying a 40-truck fleet from a retiring owner.

The prospective buyer could not meet the $1.5 million asking price and the owner, who was in her 80's, did not want to carry a second loan. "In the end, she sold the entire fleet of dump trucks and laid off all 30 employees," said Ms. Landis, of Basic Business Concepts in Pittsburgh. "No one would finance this without S.B.A. backing."

For a new business, it can be difficult to obtain even an S.B.A.–backed loan, small-business owners and bankers agree.

"It's fine and dandy," said Ms. Wade, the Virginia salon owner, "to be talking about 7(a) loans, but those are not for start-ups, they are for established businesses."

In New Mexico, Mrs. Holloway noted that it was not until she had been in business for 18 months that she was able to get a $30,000 S.B.A.–backed loan for her restaurant.

Only a tiny percentage—5.7 percent—of guaranteed loans go to rural small businesses, which is one reason Senator Snowe opposes terminating the microloan program. Fully 40 percent of microloans currently go to micro enterprises in rural areas, so her constituents in Maine would suffer if the program were shut down.

She has also criticized a proposed $85 million reduction, to $593 million, in the S.B.A.'s overall budget for fiscal 2006. Among the cutbacks she is fighting is the proposed termination of the agency's Small Business Investment Company participating securities program, which encourages venture capitalists to invest in high-technology companies.

Her counterpart in the House, Representative Donald A. Manzullo of Illinois, a Republican who leads the Small Business Committee, also has resisted administration plans to terminate the decade-old program, which, in fiscal 2004, backed more than 2,100 equity investments in small businesses by venture capitalists, totaling more than $1.4 billion.

Rich Carter, a spokesman for the House committee, said, "This program has had some hard times, but we feel we can salvage it to help small manufacturers."

Ms. Velazquez said that minority-owned ventures would be hurt most because they received, in 2004, only 11 percent of the investment company money, totaling $148 million.

Still, she predicted that the proposed cutbacks would not win approval easily in Congress, "because no one wants to be on the record as opposing small business."

The Road to Riches?

By Christopher Shea
The Boston Globe, February 29, 2004

The economy may have been flat for the last two years, but Richard Florida is soaring. The Carnegie Mellon business professor's
2002 book "The Rise of the Creative Class" connected with something in the public psyche. It heralded the arrival of a new breed of
American worker: educated, ambitious, hip, probably a mountain
biker, ready to dump a job whenever hit with the slightest urge for a
"life shift." These workers differ from the old Organization Man in
many ways, but this difference is crucial: Creative-class members
want not just decent jobs and good schools but "authentic" neighbor-
hoods, Thai food, a happening arts scene, and—most importantly—
proximity to other "creatives."

Florida's jaunty New Economy tome, a bestseller, set in motion his
thriving career as an urban-development guru. Even in the post-
boom era, civic leaders are seizing on the argument that they need
to compete not with plain old tax breaks and redevelopment
schemes, but on the playing fields of what Florida calls "the three
T's: Technology, Talent, Tolerance."

The mayor of Denver announced last fall that he'd bought copies of
"The Rise of the Creative Class" for his staff and, inspired by his
reading, engaged an $80,000-a-year public-relations expert to
"rebrand" the city as a more creative metropolis. After perusing the
book, Michigan governor Jennifer M. Granholm put on a pair of sunglasses and boasted that, thanks to Florida's ideas, Detroit, Dearborn, and Grand Rapids would soon be "so cool you'll have to wear
shades." She has asked the mayors of 250 Michigan cities and towns
to form "Cool Cities" advisory boards to brainstorm about hipster-
ization strategies. Additionally, Michigan is spreading seed money
to startups in the life sciences, high-tech automotives, and home-
land security.

Florida consults with Granholm free of charge, but he gives about
50 paid speeches a year and also owns a consulting company, Cata-
lytix, that has helped Providence, R.I., measure its "brain drain"
and is now assisting upstate New York with a revitalization plan.
(Some suggestions: Promote outdoor sports, create "support mecha-
nisms" for artists, and have local families "adopt college students"
so they'll stay in the area after graduation.) Last spring, he
appeared with leaders of Massachusetts arts groups at a two-day

conference in Framingham aimed at making the case for increased state arts funding as an engine of economic growth. Last month, he met with Hillary Clinton's staff to discuss the upstate New York plan.

Now, just as the paperback of "The Rise of the Creative Class" is appearing in bookstores, Florida is internationalizing his argument. In the current *Washington Monthly*, he argues that places like Brussels, Sydney, Wellington (think "Lord of the Rings"), and Dublin are giving American creative-tech centers a run for their money by hustling for mobile intellectual talent. Meanwhile, he writes, the Bush administration threatens to touch off a "creative class war" with innovation-busting policies like the ban on stem-cell research and increased scrutiny of foreign graduate students.

At the same time, an anti-Florida tsunami is gaining momentum. A growing number of urban-policy commentators question his advice that mayors concentrate on luring "singles, young people, homosexuals, sophistos, and trendoids," as Joel Kotkin, a journalist and professor of public policy at Pepperdine University, put it in the magazine *American Enterprise* last summer.

Florida is taking political hits from the right and the left—and battling back on his lavish website, CreativeClass.org. "There is just one problem: The basic economics behind [Florida's] ideas don't work," writes Steven Malanga in the Winter 2004 issue of the conservative *City Journal*. And in the latest issue of the waggish leftist journal the *Baffler*, based in Chicago, writer Paul Maliszewski calls Florida's city-revitalization theory "so wrong and backward that it reads like satire." Florida has "mistaken the side effects of a booming economy," he writes, "for the causes of growth." After all, "Potemkin bohemias" are not going to get old steel cities humming again.

> *"There is just one problem: The basic economics behind [Florida's] ideas don't work."*
> —Steven Malanga, writer for *City Journal*

Pepperdine's Joel Kotkin, who runs his own consulting business, says he first had his doubts about Florida's work when he read a Florida paper yoking together the Bay Area's gay-friendliness with its success as a tech incubator. "I started to think, 'San Jose is 40 miles from San Francisco and those are really different worlds,'" he says.

Then Kotkin was startled when the leaders of gray Midwestern cities began to ask him for advice on how to lure 25-year-old gay college graduates to their regions. "I'd say, 'What do you mean? You don't have a snowball's chance in hell.'" Furthermore, Kotkin dismisses Florida's idea of a 38-million-strong "creative class"—some 30 percent of the US working population—that lumps together everyone from ballerinas to software coders to accountants. "I don't see how they are more creative than bricklayers," he says.

In publications ranging from *Metropolis* to *Blueprint*, the magazine of the Democratic Leadership Council, Kotkin has been arguing that right now workers and businesses—including tech firms—are more interested in affordable housing and labor costs than they are in the availability of lattes. Besides, he argues, tech people actually like the suburbs.

Kotkin also takes issue with Florida's metrics. According to Florida, for example, San Francisco (#2), Boston (#4), and Portland (#6) are all among America's most creative cities—past and future powerhouses. But in the current issue of *Inc. Magazine*, Kotkin presents a list of the "10 Worst Metro Areas" in which to do business, which uses a more blunt measure: job creation in 2003. Boston, New York, and San Francisco, in this view, are the "lost bubble children of the 1990s": pricey and overreliant on tech.

> *"Why does New York have to play the same role in the world economy as Bangalore, or Oklahoma City?"*
> —Richard Florida, Carnegie Mellon

The top big-city job creators last year, meanwhile, were Atlanta, Riverside–San Bernardino, Las Vegas, San Antonio, and West Palm Beach—none of which are superstars according to Florida. Kotkin is especially hot on Riverside–San Bernardino, California's "Inland Empire"—a hipster urbanite's idea of sprawling hell on earth, but one which has attracted some 660,000 new residents since 1990.

In his *City Journal* article, Stephen Malanga adds some fresh attacks on Florida's statistics. Florida's list is self-contradictory, he argues: The Top 10 creative large cities increased their jobs base by 17 percent over the past decade, while his 10 worst (a roster of shame that includes Oklahoma City, New Orleans, Las Vegas, and Memphis) grew by 19 percent. The best remedies for downcast cities, Malanga argues, are the good old conservative ones: Cut taxes and slash onerous regulations.

But Florida sticks to his guns in the face of these critiques, arguing that his ideas sit squarely in the economic mainstream. He points to a long line of respectable research—by the Nobel Prize–winning economist Robert Lucas and the Harvard sociologist Daniel Bell, among others—citing the rising importance of "human capital" as America de-industrializes. Some cities may bind businesses in excessive red tape, but in the end American cities can't compete—among themselves, or worldwide—on cost alone. "Why does New York have to play the same role in the world economy as Bangalore, or Oklahoma City?" he asks.

As for Kotkin's alternate list of hot spots, Florida says: "I will take any day Boston and San Francisco and New York over Las Vegas and Des Moines and the rest of Joel's cities." The latter group, he points out, just end up manufacturing and distributing what the more "creative" cities have invented.

Can hard numbers resolve this debate? According to Harvard economist Edward Glaeser, there are grains of truth—and great dollops of hype—in both Florida's and Kotkin's views. Florida is onto something—but only in the industrial Midwest and East, where "skills are close to destiny," he thinks. (He defines skills largely as a college degree, without all the extras Florida adds.) College-educated workers, he points out, helped Boston reinvent itself after factories were shuttered.

But nationally, Glaeser believes other factors are driving growth: People want to live in sunny, dry climates and—to the horror of smart-growth advocates everywhere—they actually like car-centered cities. In place of Florida's "Technology, Talent, Tolerance," Glaeser proposes a different recipe: "Skills, Sun, Sprawl."

The most biting attack on Florida comes, ironically, on class grounds. When Pittsburgh razes an old factory, the *Baffler*'s Paul Maliszewski charges, Richard Florida gets teary over the loss of future loft apartments, while the steelworkers who've lost their jobs over the last quarter-century are acknowledged "only in passing and as statistics." In Florida's new utopia, the working class exists only to "serve the creatives, cleaning up their mess." In a C-SPAN exchange acidly described by Maliszewski, entrepreneurs with "idle minds and comfortable bodies" whine to Florida that unions and taxes are hampering their deep creative visions.

Florida, who has posted a lengthy rebuttal to the *Baffler* on his website, calls this attack "really weird." He says he is constantly telling city fathers that they need to harness the creative power of all their citizens, rich and poor. "What we have to do is open up membership in the creative class to a much greater group of people," he says, until it eventually includes "everyone."

So schools need to get better, for starters. Admittedly, that's not quite as catchy as the soundbites Florida was generating two years ago, but at least it's one even squares can get behind.

III. American Jobs and the Global Economy

Editor's Introduction

When treated as a set of broad economic issues, jobs can seem almost abstract. Economists and policy experts survey and evaluate them; governments sprinkle tax money here and there in hopes of cultivating them. But thinking of employment in these terms obscures the individual people who have to find, take, leave, or lose every job being discussed. In "North of the Border," the second article in this section, the economist Paul Krugman quotes the mid-20th-century Swiss playwright Max Frisch as saying, apropos Switzerland's troubled attempt to manage immigration, "We wanted a labor force, but human beings came." As Frisch's comment suggests, immigration and outsourcing, the primary issues under scrutiny in this chapter, might be divisive precisely because they highlight conflicts between abstract American ideals—such as the notion of a welcoming country full of people with differing backgrounds brought together in part by a shared respect for the principles of free enterprise—and the unavoidable reality that differences exist and that marketplace efficiency can come at the expense of particular people or places.

There can be little question that immigration and outsourcing are among the most divisive economic issues currently under debate in the United States. Positions on immigration are particularly freighted with labels—such as conservative and liberal, or Republican and Democrat—that indicate virtually nothing about where the people holding those positions might stand. An example of how immigration defies conventional political categories can be seen in this chapter's first two entries—both written by esteemed professors, from perspectives that might be broadly described as liberal—though the ideas about immigration they express are clearly distinct. In the first selection, "Closed-Door Policy," sociologist Douglas S. Massey presents immigration, particularly from Mexico, as a natural and necessary outgrowth of a shared border and long-standing economic ties and calls for a rational and consistent policy for regulating immigrants' entry and return. Krugman, on the other hand, acknowledges being "instinctively, emotionally pro-immigration" but finds himself troubled by "a review of serious, nonpartisan research" on the topic. Krugman cites studies suggesting that the influx of low-skilled immigrant labor has led to a decline in wages among similarly skilled Americans and argues that "low-skill immigrants don't pay enough taxes to cover the cost of the benefits they receive."

Krugman and Massey concern themselves with only part of the immigration phenomenon, however. In "Made in America," Sarah Childress highlights the increasing number of businesses founded by immigrants, particularly immigrant women. June Kronholz's article "Businesses Push for High-Skilled Foreign Workers" sheds light on the intense demand for immigrants, many of them products of the American education system, who possess the specialized skills that businesses seek.

The next two selections offer concrete information on a topic often treated anecdotally: outsourcing. While in its broadest sense the word designates only one company's use of another company's services, the term has increasingly come to suggest the reliance on foreign labor to perform work that, until that time, had been done by Americans. In "Savior or Villain?" Timothy Aeppel considers outsourcing through the lens of a single Illinois town, where the economic base is shifting from manufacturing to the service industry, a transformation symbolized by the opening of a more than 20-acre warehouse for the retail chain Wal-Mart. The next article, written by Doug Henwood and appearing originally in the left-wing magazine the *Nation* as part of a special section entitled "Toward a Progressive View on Outsourcing," reviews some of the hard data on American jobs lost to outsourcing and finds that, compared to other economic issues, outsourcing "is a diversion."

Though currently not discussed as passionately as immigration or outsourcing, the North American Free Trade Agreement (NAFTA) and its effect on American jobs have engendered intense debate since the years before its implementation in January 1994. In the final entry in this chapter, Terry Kosdrosky looks at how NAFTA has affected people in a city that for decades was the country's most famous manufacturing hub, Detroit. What the author finds is suggested in the article's title: "A Mixed Result."

Closed-Door Policy

By Douglas S. Massey
American Prospect, July/August 2003

At the dawn of the 21st century, the United States offers a contradictory model of global economic openness. American policy has relentlessly promoted open commerce, leading the way by freeing its own markets to foreign investment, trade and travel. America's own borders have become increasingly open for flows of capital, goods, commodities, information and certain favored classes of people: entrepreneurs, scientists, students, tourists and corporate employees. When it comes to the movement of ordinary labor, however, America has not sought openness. Rather, the thrust of U.S. policy since the 1950s has been to make it more difficult for workers to enter the United States in search of jobs, except via narrow programs under corporate control.

This contradiction is nowhere more apparent than in U.S. relations with Mexico, which together with Canada is our largest trading partner. Since 1986, U.S. officials have worked closely with officials in both countries to create an integrated North American economy, open to flows of goods, capital, commodities, services and information. Yet within this integrated economy we somehow, magically, do not want any labor to be moving. Against all logic, we wish to create an integrated, continent-wide economy characterized by the free movement of all factors of production except one.

This schizophrenia is manifest in the fact that, since the mid-1980s, we have moved in two diametrically opposed directions, at once promoting integration while simultaneously seeking separation. Between 1985 and 2000, total trade between Mexico and the United States increased by a factor of eight, the number of Mexican tourists quintupled, Mexican business visitors and intra-company transferees tripled, and the total number of persons crossing the border for short visits doubled. All this came about according to plan, and only intensified with enactment of the North American Free Trade Agreement.

At the same time, however, U.S. officials have sought to maintain the illusion of separation. As trade expanded between 1985 and 2000, U.S. spending on border enforcement increased by a factor of six, the number of U.S. Border Patrol officers doubled and hours spent by agents patrolling the frontier tripled. During the 1990s, two of the top 10 fastest growing job categories in the federal workforce were "Immigration Inspector" and "Border Patrol Agent." Today the Border Patrol is the largest arms-bearing branch of the U.S. government except for the military itself, with a budget well in excess of $1 billion per year. In many border communities, the Immigration and Naturalization Service is now the largest employer.

Why has the United States chosen to militarize a peaceful border with its closest trading partner, a democratic country that poses no conceivable threat to U.S. security? The answer, I fear, rests on seriously mistaken notions about the nature of immigration in today's postindustrial, globalized economy.

The most basic misconception is that, without a heavily militarized border, the United States will be invaded by an army of destitute immigrants fleeing abject poverty, or flooded by a tidal wave of poor foreigners eager to take Americans' jobs and consume public services at taxpayer expense. Politicians—liberal as well as conservative—find the imagery of invasions and floods useful during periods of economic insecurity and rising inequality, for it deflects attention from more fundamental questions about the distribution

---

The truth is that most immigrants to the United States are not desperate people fleeing poverty and social chaos overseas.

---

of wealth and power in the United States. Immigrants provide a convenient scapegoat to absorb voter anger about the erosion of wages, the instability of unemployment and declining access to social benefits. Politicians and the media periodically manufacture immigration and border crises as the need arises, and the restrictiveness of immigration policies is inversely correlated with the business cycle.

The truth is that most immigrants to the United States are not desperate people fleeing poverty and social chaos overseas. International migration is a well-ordered process connected to broader processes of global trade, geopolitical integration and market expansion; it is simply the labor component of a globalizing market economy. Developed nations that receive flows of capital, goods, services and commodities also receive immigrants. As a result, western Europe, Japan, Korea, Singapore and other countries have joined traditional immigrant-receiving nations such as the United States, Canada and Australia to become net importers of labor.

The poorest and most populous nations of the world, with a large share of those who have the most to gain from international migration, generally do not send the most migrants. If emigration were caused by poverty, most immigrants would come from Africa, followed by the Caribbean, Asia and Latin America. Among immigrants to the United States during the 1990s, however, just 3 percent came from Africa whereas 11 percent came from the Caribbean, 30 percent from Asia and 36 percent from Latin America. Likewise, the rate of international migration across countries bears no relation whatsoever to the rate of demographic increase: The correlation is virtually zero.

Among sending countries, emigration does not stem from a lack of development but from development itself. International migration has always been part and parcel of broader processes of economic growth and development. In the course of its industrialization, for example, Europe exported 54 million people. Emigrants are created by social and economic transformations in societies undergoing rapid change as a result of their incorporation into the global market economy. What is remarkable about today's developing nations is not that they produce emigrants but that they produce so few. Whereas Britain ended up exporting half of its population increase in the course of its development, South Korea exported less than 5 percent of its demographic increase. At present, fewer than 3 percent of the world's people live outside their countries of birth.

Nor are those who do leave their countries of origin in search of work overseas the poorest of citizens. Indeed, labor emigrants tend to be drawn from the middle of a country's socioeconomic distribution, not the bottom. When they go, moreover, migrants typically do not go to nations that are richest or closest. Rather, they proceed along established pathways to countries that are already connected politically, socially and economically to their countries of origin. The main sources of immigrants for the United States are thus its closest trading partners (Mexico, Canada, China), former colonies (the Philippines, Puerto Rico), and regions where the United States has recently intervened militarily or politically (Central America, the Caribbean, Southeast Asia).

That Mexico is by far the largest source of U.S. immigrants is hardly surprising. In addition to sharing a land border with the United States, it was twice invaded by U.S. troops in the 20th century (in 1914 and 1917), it has been the target of two U.S.–sponsored labor recruitment efforts (during 1917–18 and 1942–64), and since 1986, at U.S. insistence, it has undertaken a radical transformation of its political economy and entered the global market. Moreover, since 1994 it has been linked to the United States by NAFTA, a comprehensive economic treaty that presently generates $250 billion per year in binational trade.

Under these circumstances, immigration between the two countries is inevitable, even though Mexico is wealthy by Third World standards. With a per capita gross domestic product of $9,000, it is one of the richest countries in Latin America. It is in the interest of the United States, therefore, to build on this economic base by accepting Mexican immigration as a reality and working to manage it in a way that minimizes the costs and maximizes the benefits for both nations.

The repressive border controls imposed by the United States since 1986 have done precisely the opposite, however. Studies have found no discernable effect of restrictive immigration policies on the inflow of Mexican immigrants, documented or undocumented. Indeed, during the 1990s, a record 2.2 million Mexican immigrants entered the country legally, constituting a quarter of all documented immigration. At the same time, the probability of apprehension for undocumented migrants fell to record-low levels, raising the odds of their ultimately gaining access. By the mid-1990s, the probability of apprehension had fallen to as low as 20 percent per attempt. The selective concentration of enforcement resources at specific locations along the border redirected migratory flows toward other sectors where fewer Border Patrol officers were stationed. Perversely, more people actually got in.

By redirecting migrants toward more remote and inhospitable sectors, the selective hardening of the border tripled the rate of border mortality, causing hundreds of needless deaths each year. Moreover, as a result of the increased risks of entering the United States, Mexican migrants rationally chose to minimize border crossings, not by remaining home but by staying longer once they got in. Paradoxically, the principal effect of border militarization has been to reduce the odds of going home, not of coming in the first place.

As the size of the return flow plummeted during the 1990s, it produced a spectacular and unprecedented increase in the Mexican population of the United States. The wall of enforcement resources erected after 1993 was especially high in San Diego, which deflected migrants away from California and toward other regions of the country. Whereas 63 percent of all Mexicans who arrived between 1985 and 1990 went to California, just 35 percent of those arriving between 1995 and 2000 did so, creating an explosion of Mexican populations in a host of new receiving states.

In addition to increasing the size of the Mexican population and spreading it throughout the United States, U.S. policies have marginalized immigrants socially and economically. The criminalization of undocumented hiring in 1986 caused employers to shift from direct employment to labor subcontracting. In the wake of this legislation, everyone who wished to work in certain sectors of the labor market—agriculture, gardening, construction, custodial services— had to go through a subcontractor. It didn't matter if they were legal residents or citizens. The subcontractor, of course, took a cut of their wages as payment, money that before 1986 would have gone to the immigrants themselves. The net effect was to reduce the wages and undermine the working conditions not of undocumented migrants but of U.S. workers.

Other laws passed in 1996 stripped legal immigrants of the right to certain social entitlements, causing a stampede toward naturalization. More naturalizations mean more immigrants at a later date, because a U.S. citizen can sponsor the entry of spouses, unmarried sons and daughters, and parents without restriction. In addition, citizens may petition for the entry of adult sons and daughters, as well as for brothers and sisters, subject to numerical limitation. Each new citizen thus creates a host of legal entitlements for additional immigration.

At the same time, a large fraction of new immigrants are undocumented and marginalized from the rest of American society; even those with legal papers find their access to social benefits constrained unless they are citizens.

Repressive border policies make it more difficult for migrants to achieve their ambition of returning home.

If U.S. authorities had set out to intentionally design a program to create a future underclass, they could not have done a better job.

The fundamental problem with U.S. immigration policy toward Mexico—and with U.S. immigration policy generally—is that it treats international migration as a pathological condition to be repressed through unilateral actions. In reality, immigration is the natural outgrowth of broader processes of market expansion and economic integration that can be managed for the mutual advantage of trading partners. By migrating in response to structural adjustments at home, migrants generally do not intend to remain abroad for the rest of their lives. Some do, of course, and others change their mind as a result of their experience in the host society. But left to their own devices, most would return home, for they are migrating not to maximize income but to overcome economic problems at home. They use international migration instrumentally as a way of overcoming the missing and failed markets that are quite common in the course of economic development. The money they earn abroad is repatriated in the form of savings and remittances, which total around $60 billion worldwide. Repressive border policies make it more difficult for migrants to achieve their ambition of returning home.

Rather than accepting immigration as a logical consequence of America's hegemonic position at the core of a global market economy, U.S. political leaders have enacted repressive unilateral policies to create the impression that immigration is not occurring, that U.S. borders are "under control" and that U.S. citizens are protected from the presumed ill effects of immigrants. In fact, such policies achieve the opposite: Immigration continues, but in a way that undermines the status and welfare of U.S. residents.

Before September 11, presidents George W. Bush and Vicente Fox appeared to be moving toward an agreement to manage Mexican labor migration by expanding the quota for legal immigrants, creating a reasonable temporary-worker program, facilitating the return of migrants and the investment of their dollars, and regularizing the status of undocumented Mexicans in the United

States. Unfortunately, the 9-11 hijackers derailed this negotiation and President Fox was left standing at the border looking northward with his hand extended as President Bush turned his back to launch the war on terrorism.

In the end, the Bush administration must learn that national security involves more than toppling ruthless dictators in distant lands. It also requires attending to the political stability and economic security of a country of 100 million people with whom we share a 2,000 mile border. The administration's inattention to migration in the context of North American integration has undermined the statute and standing of Mexico's first democratically elected president in 70 years. And every day that passes without a labor agreement makes it more difficult for Mexico to realize its full potential for economic growth.

The answer is not open borders, of course, but frontiers that are reasonably regulated on a binational basis. At present, all countries have the same quota of 20,000 legal immigrants per year, no matter their size or relationship to the United States. Thus, our largest and closest neighbor and most important trading partner has the same limited access to U.S. visas as Botswana, Nepal and Paraguay. A more realistic policy would recognize Mexico's unique status by increasing the annual immigrant quota, establishing a flexible temporary labor program and regularizing the status of those already here.

By bringing the flows above board, we would mitigate the downward pressures on wages and working conditions in the United States while raising tax revenues that could be used to offset the costs of immigration and to assist Mexico in overcoming the market failures that motivate so many moves north of the border. If we cannot manage migratory exchanges with Mexico as it joins with us to create an integrated North American market, how can we possibly hope to manage the migratory flows that will be coming from China as it is transformed by participating in the global market economy?

North of the Border

BY PAUL KRUGMAN
THE NEW YORK TIMES, MARCH 27, 2006

"Give me your tired, your poor, your huddled masses yearning to breathe free," wrote Emma Lazarus, in a poem that still puts a lump in my throat. I'm proud of America's immigrant history, and grateful that the door was open when my grandparents fled Russia.

In other words, I'm instinctively, emotionally pro-immigration. But a review of serious, nonpartisan research reveals some uncomfortable facts about the economics of modern immigration, and immigration from Mexico in particular. If people like me are going to respond effectively to anti-immigrant demagogues, we have to acknowledge those facts.

First, the net benefits to the U.S. economy from immigration, aside from the large gains to the immigrants themselves, are small. Realistic estimates suggest that immigration since 1980 has raised the total income of native-born Americans by no more than a fraction of 1 percent.

Second, while immigration may have raised overall income slightly, many of the worst-off native-born Americans are hurt by immigration—especially immigration from Mexico. Because Mexican immigrants have much less education than the average U.S. worker, they increase the supply of less-skilled labor, driving down the wages of the worst-paid Americans. The most authoritative recent study of this effect, by George Borjas and Lawrence Katz of Harvard, estimates that U.S. high school dropouts would earn as much as 8 percent more if it weren't for Mexican immigration.

That's why it's intellectually dishonest to say, as President Bush does, that immigrants do "jobs that Americans will not do." The willingness of Americans to do a job depends on how much that job pays—and the reason some jobs pay too little to attract native-born Americans is competition from poorly paid immigrants.

Finally, modern America is a welfare state, even if our social safety net has more holes in it than it should—and low-skill immigrants threaten to unravel that safety net.

Basic decency requires that we provide immigrants, once they're here, with essential health care, education for their children, and more. As the Swiss writer Max Frisch wrote about his own country's experience with immigration, "We wanted a labor force, but human beings came." Unfortunately, low-skill immigrants don't pay enough taxes to cover the cost of the benefits they receive.

Worse yet, immigration penalizes governments that act humanely. Immigrants are a much more serious fiscal problem in California than in Texas, which treats the poor and unlucky harshly, regardless of where they were born.

We shouldn't exaggerate these problems. Mexican immigration, says the Borjas-Katz study, has played only a "modest role" in growing U.S. inequality. And the political threat that low-skill immigration poses to the welfare state is more serious than the fiscal threat: the disastrous Medicare drug bill alone does far more to undermine the finances of our social insurance system than the whole burden of dealing with illegal immigrants.

But modest problems are still real problems, and immigration is becoming a major political issue. What are we going to do about it?

Realistically, we'll need to reduce the inflow of low-skill immigrants. Mainly that means better controls on illegal immigration. But the harsh anti-immigration legislation passed by the House, which has led to huge protests—legislation that would, among other things, make it a criminal act to provide an illegal immigrant with medical care—is simply immoral.

Meanwhile, Mr. Bush's plan for a "guest worker" program is clearly designed by and for corporate interests, who'd love to have a low-wage work force that couldn't vote. Not only is it deeply un-American; it does nothing to reduce the adverse effect of immigration on wages. And because guest workers would face the prospect of deportation after a few years, they would have no incentive to become integrated into our society.

What about a guest-worker program that includes a clearer route to citizenship? I'd still be careful. Whatever the bill's intentions, it could all too easily end up having the same effect as the Bush plan in practice—that is, it could create a permanent underclass of disenfranchised workers.

We need to do something about immigration, and soon. But I'd rather see Congress fail to agree on anything this year than have it rush into ill-considered legislation that betrays our moral and democratic principles.

Made in America

By Sarah Childress
Newsweek, November 14, 2005

Sheela Murthy, who moved to the United States from India in 1986, had worked only a few years at a New York law firm when she glimpsed her own glass ceiling. "It just felt like, 'Why am I here at 2 in the morning, photocopying documents?'" she says. Murthy remembers thinking of the American Dream, "If this is really real, why don't I pluck some of the golden fruit?" After trying another firm in Baltimore, she started her own, specializing in immigration law. For a month she sat at home, making cold calls. Eleven years later, her firm had swelled to 11 lawyers. Now Murthy's found her dream job—and is making more money than she ever had at the copy machine.

Immigrant women are steadily carving out space for themselves in the world's biggest economies. In the past decade, the number of immigrant women business owners in the United States exploded by nearly 200 percent, according to a study by the Immigration Policy Center in Washington, D.C. The percentage of self-employed immigrant women is higher than the corresponding number of self-employed native-born women, and they're even closing the gap with immigrant men. Their entrepreneurialism is partly pragmatic: by working on their own terms, immigrant women can earn extra money without struggling in a hostile workplace or worrying about child care. But it's also a sign of a changing world. More female immigrants have better education and skills than before, and it is increasingly acceptable for them to work outside the home.

Most of their businesses are small start-ups in which women sell products they learned to make in their native countries. That's how Ofelia Nieto, 39, a Colombian refugee who arrived in the United States with her family two years ago, became an entrepreneur. She started selling handmade necklaces to her California neighbors to help pay the bills. Now she hawks her wares at local fairs, hotels and boutiques—and is working on expanding online. Others manage day-care services, or run restaurants and beauty salons. And increasingly, women are expanding into other industries, like real estate, tech consulting and even construction.

What drives a newcomer to an unfamiliar land to start her own business? Susan Pearce, who conducted the Immigration Policy Center's study, says lower-class women are often "pushed" into entrepreneurship when they find they need more than one job to support a family. Those who don't speak the language can't find a job in the traditional workplace. Women from wealthy, educated families are "pulled" by the promise of fulfilling dreams they could never have realized in their native countries.

Banks and other groups are recognizing the potential and reaching out. In the past, most women got start-up capital from family members. Thanks to anti-discrimination provisions and micro-enterprise loans for small businesses, that's starting to change. Nonprofit groups have stepped in to help immigrant business owners. Several state chapters of the International Rescue Committee in the United States, for example, offer micro-enterprise programs that help with everything from making business cards and setting up a Web site to securing loans and customers.

Governments elsewhere have started to reach out, too, with programs to help would-be entrepreneurs navigate foreign regulations and to offer support. When Nousha Pakpour, who is now in her 60s, immigrated to England from Iran in 1978, she left behind two hair salons and her own hairdressing school. But with broken English and no work visa, the best she could manage in London was a job shampooing hair and sweeping the floors. Eventually she turned to fashion, obtained a loan from the British government and opened a boutique. It was a thriving business for four years, until she abandoned it to start the Lady's Creative Centre, an organization that helps immigrant women tap into their own creative talent to form businesses.

U.S. experts predict that the number of women entrepreneurs will only continue to rise, strengthening the support network for other newcomers. "It's not only their success that's important to the economy, it's the trickle-down," says Pearce. "They're employing people, ensuring that we have an educated, healthy next generation that's going to grow up and commit to our labor force." Chances are, they'll be doing a lot more than making photocopies.

Businesses Push for High-Skilled Foreign Workers

BY JUNE KRONHOLZ
THE WALL STREET JOURNAL, APRIL 6, 2006

Last year, Stanford University awarded 88 Ph.D.s in electrical engineering, 49 of which went to foreign-born students. U.S. business would like to hang on to these kinds of prized graduates and not lose them to the world—which is one reason why it has a big stake in the immigration bill that is consuming the Senate.

The fate of millions of illegal immigrants, most of them low-skilled workers, dominates that debate. But the future of thousands of high-skilled foreign workers seeking admission to the country—scientists, mathematicians, health-care workers—may be equally important to the U.S. economy. Because of the key role many of those workers play in cutting-edge businesses, industry lobbyists are pushing measures that would more than double the number of visas available to skilled workers.

But if the years-long effort to overhaul the U.S. immigration system collapses, the issue of those visas could be buried in the rubble. "Our biggest fear is that the other issue—the undocumented workers—bogs down and threatens the entire bill," says Ralph Hellman of the Information Technology Industry Council, a Washington-based trade group.

President Bush waded into the fray Wednesday, urging senators to come to a quick conclusion, and Democrats were invited into what had been Republican-only meetings to find a compromise that can win the 60 votes needed to close debate. More talks will be held Thursday between Sens. Edward Kennedy (D., Mass.) and John McCain (R., Ariz.). But last evening, Majority Leader Bill Frist (R., Tenn.) was already moving to introduce a new Republican plan to address the legal status of undocumented workers in the U.S.

Those who arrived before April 2001 could begin an arduous but clear 11-year path to citizenship similar to that outlined in the Senate Judiciary Committee bill reported last week. But to appease conservatives, those who have come in the past five years are promised less.

In fact, anyone who can't prove that he or she was here legally before January 2004 would risk deportation, while a third, middle group of people who arrived in the intervening years could enter a temporary worker program. The annual cap on the number of visas for the program in the underlying Judiciary bill would be waived for these workers, but a Frist aide said they would be required within three years to get their paperwork in order, go to a port of entry of the U.S. and re-enter legally with a work permit.

As seen in the current talks, increasing visa limits for workers at all skill levels is certain to be part of any future compromise. Business is eager for more low-skilled immigration to keep the service and construction industries humming, but it's also lobbying hard for workers for high-tech and science-based industries.

Currently, only 65,000 three-year visas are available to skilled workers each year, and demand for those slots was so strong in the fiscal year that started in October 2005 that employers, who must sponsor those workers, snapped up all of them by last August.

U.S.–born students account for only about half the science, math, technology and engineering advanced-degree holders turned out by American universities yearly.

The government also gives out 140,000 employment-based visas yearly—so-called green cards that put immigrants on the track to citizenship. But those visas are shared equally among all sending countries. That means that an employer hoping to hire a Chinese- or Indian-born worker now has at least a five-year wait before the immigration service even reads the application.

Employers from hospitals to high schools increasingly are reliant on foreign workers who enter the U.S. through the employment-visa line. But high-tech employers are particularly dependent, and they say that the paucity of visas threatens their competitiveness.

Dallas-based Texas Instruments Inc. says about 500 of its 19,000 domestic employees are waiting for U.S. green cards, and that most of them are electrical engineers. Those workers are in the U.S. on temporary work permits, but while their green-card applications are pending, they can't change work assignments or cities to meet their companies' needs.

Employers are particularly irked by the visa system's treatment of foreign-born scientists who must leave the country after finishing their studies if a U.S. company can't secure a visa to hire them. As it is, U.S.–born students account for only about half the science, math, technology and engineering advanced-degree holders turned out by American universities yearly.

When companies run out of U.S.–born workers, and then can't hire immigrants, "projects get dropped or delayed, so development is slowed down," says Patrick Duffy, a human-resources lawyer for Intel Corp.

"It's not as if the work won't get done, it's where will the work get done," adds Sandra Boyd, who heads a National Association of Manufacturers competitiveness initiative.

In 1999, at the height of the dot-com bubble, high-tech industries convinced Congress to triple the number of temporary visas available every year. That largely met the economy's needs, says the Information Technology council. But the measure expired in 2003, and with the high-tech industry then ailing, employers didn't push for an extension.

Two years ago, under renewed pressure from employers, Congress made a modest adjustment. It exempted 20,000 advanced-degree holders who already were studying at U.S. universities from the cap on temporary visas, allowing them to take jobs with U.S. employers. But again, demand was so strong that those slots were filled on Jan. 9 for the fiscal year beginning in October.

"It doesn't make sense to educate this talent and then send them to our global competition to compete against us," says Intel's Mr. Duffy.

Lobbyists for the technology industry say they get a sympathetic hearing on Capitol Hill with that argument. The immigration bill passed by the Senate Judiciary Committee last week increases the number of green cards to 290,000 and the number of temporary visas to 115,000.

It also exempts U.S.–educated advanced-degree holders in science, technology, engineering and math from both of those caps, and puts them on an immediate path to citizenship, if they choose to stay in the U.S. after finishing their degrees.

An immigration bill passed by the House in December focuses on enforcing immigration laws on the border and in workplaces.

But the Information Technology council's Mr. Hellman says he expects that House members who are appointed to the conference committee that reconciles the House and Senate versions of any immigration bills will support measures aimed at high-skilled workers.

If that compromise bill does more than just enhance enforcement, he says, "our (issue) is first in line in terms of support."

But Congress might not get that far. Absent some agreement this morning between Sens. McCain and Kennedy, the Senate splits over undocumented workers now appear headed toward two cloture votes—neither of which will succeed to cut off debate on the Judiciary bill and Mr. Frist's new alternative. "I cannot see the end of the tunnel to know if there is a light there," said Judiciary Chairman Arlen Specter (R., Pa.) Wednesday night.

If that happens, industry lobbyists say they would try to attach their visa measures to a spending bill later in the year. That risks further delay and uncertainty, though, even while competitors, including Britain, are streamlining their immigration systems to attract high-skilled workers. "We'll find ourselves playing catch-up," warns the National Association of Manufacturers' Ms. Boyd.

Savior or Villain?

By Timothy Aeppel
The Wall Street Journal, February 24, 2006

When Leo Wahl patented "vibrator motor hair clippers" in 1924, a steel mill belched smoke along the Rock River here [in Sterling, IL] and nearby factories churned out hinges, nails and chicken wire.

Today, Wahl Clipper Corp. is the last of Sterling's home-grown, family-run manufacturers. Most of the others have either shut down or shriveled in recent years, in part, because of intense pressure from big-box retailers for rock-bottom prices.

Shoppers at the big Wal-Mart store just a few miles from Wahl's tidy factory on North Locust Street can still find the familiar local name stamped on boxes there, but nearly all the lower-priced items, such as nose-hair clippers and curling irons, are shipped across the Pacific Ocean from China.

"I think pricing pressure is probably the single biggest dynamic that is pushing people to go to China," says Greg Wahl, chief executive of Wahl and grandson of the founder. Wahl uses some imported components to make many higher-end products in Sterling but built four foreign plants, including its largest in Ningbo, China, to help keep the business of chains like Wal-Mart, the company's biggest retail customer.

It's the most daunting challenge facing U.S. manufacturers and the communities that depend upon them: How do you stay alive when so many things seem to be made so much cheaper someplace else? Not unlike Wahl Clipper, the answer for Sterling has been to embrace the changing world, where a retailer like Wal-Mart, whose fierce cost-cutting has been blamed for driving jobs overseas, can be as much a savior as a villain.

Next month, with the opening of an 880,000-square-foot warehouse next to a freeway on-ramp on the outskirts of town, Wal-Mart Stores Inc. will become Sterling's largest employer.

"People talk about the irony of it, but at the end of the day, we live in a free economy where everyone has to adapt," says Peter Dillon, a community leader who helped land the Wal-Mart facility and whose family owned the steel mill until 1988.

Susan Adami is among those adapting. She recently started work in quality control at the new distribution center after 29 years at a hinge factory that recently announced it was shifting nearly all production to China.

Ms. Adami, who is 47 years old, began working in a hinge factory straight out of high school, when manufacturing jobs were considered a secure stepping stone to a comfortable life. But for years, she's listened to managers gripe about global pressures that were forcing cutbacks—in vacation days, health benefits, and paychecks. When she was offered the Wal-Mart job, the interviewer asked if the $13 an hour starting pay was appealing. She had to catch herself, she says.

"I wanted to tell them, 'Heck, that's more than I've made working 29 years,'" she says. Her last job paid $11 an hour, the most she ever earned working in a factory. She recently went to Texas for a two-week training stint at a Wal-Mart distribution center identical to the one being built in Sterling.

A Wal-Mart spokesman says some 6,000 people have applied for the 675 jobs, which range from forklift drivers and benefits clerks to maintenance workers. The workers at the distribution center will get a minimum of $13 an hour, with a premium for those like Ms. Adami, who work a compressed three-day, weekend shift. Certain skilled workers earn $16 an hour or more. Wal-Mart declines to say what it pays the 375 employees of its Sterling store, noting instead that the average pay for such workers in Illinois is $10.41 an hour.

Long-time Sterling resident Kevin Heller, 44, has mixed feelings about Wal-Mart. As the son of a mill worker, he sees Wal-Mart's cost-squeezing as part of the reason jobs have left. "But if I separate out those feelings, I'm ecstatic," he says, "because I'm a bill collector—so it's good to get these people back to work."

Mr. Heller's collections agency has already seen an uptick in business over the past few months, with laid off workers calling to say they have landed jobs at Wal-Mart and are preparing to resume paying down debts.

Wal-Mart's local boosters emphasize that the situation would be far worse without it. And, indeed, there are plenty of signs of Sterling's economic woes. The preliminary unemployment rate of 5.9% in December was well above the national average. The share of patients treated at the local hospital who are on public assistance jumped to 13% from 8% since 2001, while the bills of "charity cases"—working poor who can't afford treatment—has tripled in that time to $3 million. And Sterling's schools have had to cut sports programs and other extracurricular activities in response to a budget squeeze.

The town's population has held steady at about 15,000 for the past decade, even as a half dozen large factories have closed or drastically downsized, costing thousands of jobs. But the makeup of the population is shifting. Some homes are starting to be snapped up by people moving out to escape Chicago's lofty housing market, about

100 miles to the east. Meanwhile, many younger skilled workers and professionals are moving away in search of work, many local residents say.

The town's biggest problem used to be labor shortages. In the late 1950s, one of Mr. Dillon's first jobs for his family's mill included traveling to barber shops within a 30-mile radius, tacking up signs pleading for workers to come to Sterling.

During the boom after World War II, the mill even sent recruiters into Mexico, providing temporary housing for these newcomers in a cluster of silver railway cars which locals dubbed the Silver City. Today, Sterling's population is 18% Hispanic, many of them factory workers and their children lured to town during that postwar heyday.

Jesus Frias is one of them. His father came to Illinois from Mexico as a farm worker, but saw the good-paying jobs for immigrants in Sterling's factories and encouraged his son to follow him north.

Many manufacturers . . . don't pay a big premium compared to other types of unskilled and semiskilled work.

Mr. Frias, 50, spent 28 years in a hardware plant, but recently accepted a job at the new Wal-Mart distribution center, where he is scheduled to start March 20th. Asked if Wal-Mart is a better job, he says it's hard to tell. "I hope they do OK. I'm just going to take a chance and go out there."

The evolution of Sterling, which once styled itself the nation's Hardware Capital, echoes a larger economic change in the U.S. industrial heartland, as certain types of factory jobs dwindle and regions look anxiously toward the future. Manufacturing remains a good way to make a living. The average annual wage for full-time U.S. factory workers is $48,731, compared to $28,216 in retailing and $19,934 in hotels, two of the economy's fastest growing sectors. Factory work also offers relatively rich benefits.

But these figures mask an uneven reality. Many manufacturers, especially those facing foreign competition, don't pay a big premium compared to other types of unskilled and semiskilled work.

Lawrence Brothers, the oldest hardware maker in town, went bankrupt in 2001, while National Manufacturing Co. was just bought by New Britain, Conn.–based Stanley Works. Four years ago, National produced 80% of its hardware in Sterling, importing the rest from cheaper producers overseas. Now, domestic production has dropped to 50%, and in the next year it will fall to 40%, according to company managers.

The biggest jolt, however, was the bankruptcy of Northwestern Steel & Wire Co. in 2001, which meant the sudden loss of 1,500 jobs. As a unionized steelmaker and producer of wire products, Northwestern had long anchored the top of the local blue-collar pay scale, creating pressure on other manufacturers to pay more than they might otherwise. A Missouri company bought part of the old mill and has restarted it, though it only employs about 250.

Mr. Dillon, a board member of the Greater Sterling Development Corp., says landing the Wal-Mart distribution center was an "outstanding achievement." But even he has mixed feelings about the broader changes in Sterling's economy. "I'd rather see us adding high-paying manufacturing jobs," he says, which are more likely to create wealth in the long-term.

Marty Heires, a Wal-Mart spokesman, says the company opens two or three distribution centers a year, which often become the focal point for further economic development, such as truck stops and retail stores.

"This is a sustainable model where we pay good wages and good benefits," Mr. Heires says. "Will all the associates in this facility become independently wealthy entrepreneurs? No. But they'll make a good wage. We can pay a lot of taxes. We can attract complementary businesses to the community and we feel that can have a long and dramatic impact on a community like Sterling, Ill."

Beyond the dollars and cents, a sense of obligation to the community still runs deep in the old families. Mr. Dillon heads the $84 million Dillon Foundation, which focuses on local charities and community projects. And the Wahls are a major benefactor of the local Roman Catholic diocese. The Bensons, one of the founding families of National Manufacturing, are avid supporters of the YMCA and the local hospital.

At Wahl Clipper's Sterling plant, 650 workers cut and polish blades, mold colorful plastic casings, and assemble machines used by barbers, dog groomers, and surgeons all over the world. While that's down from a peak of 804 Sterling-based employees in 1997, Mr. Wahl, 54 and the fourth Wahl to lead the company, says he can't see moving more offshore. Having a domestic presence keeps the company linked to its customers and aids quick response to new product innovations, he says.

Mr. Wahl says there are many factors—not just cost—driving manufacturers abroad, including the growing need to be close to China's rapidly expanding base of suppliers. By contrast, Mr. Wahl says that by having its own factories overseas rather than contracting with manufacturers there gives his company an advantage. "I think having more control over our whole supply chain puts us in a better position," he says. "It means that when Wal-Mart wants something low-cost, they can buy directly from us; whereas with our competitors, they're buying from a middleman."

Leading the way into the back of the factory, Mr. Wahl stops by a pallet stacked with boxes of professional-grade clippers. The destination marked on the side: Brazil.

"You have to decide how you're going to be successful," he says. "I believe doing the right thing for our employees and our customers is where our profit comes from."

He says Wahl Clipper just finished its best year ever.

Toward a Progressive View on Outsourcing

By Doug Henwood
The Nation, March 22, 2004

Whatever happened to the once-touted Great American Jobs Machine? Lately it seems to have popped a gasket. More than 700,000 jobs disappeared between the official end of the recession in November 2001 and January 2004 (the latest month available), unprecedented behavior during a supposed economic recovery. Where'd they go?

Abroad, is the standard answer, to factories in China and call centers in Bangalore. "Outsourcing" and "offshoring" are the polite ways of putting it, the words preferred by consultants and pundits. In the cruder version, it's "foreigners are stealing our jobs." In the mainstream, the major difference of opinion is whether this is a good thing or not in the long term. The President's top economic adviser, Gregory Mankiw, got into some seriously hot water the other week for saying that the phenomenon represented only the "latest manifestation of the gains from trade that economists have talked about" since the days of Ricardo, two centuries ago. To Ralph Nader and the Democratic presidential candidates, it's a bad thing that explains much of the job market's ills, one of the issues they hope to ride into the White House. Most progressives accept the analysis. The problem is that it doesn't seem to be true.

Let's look at some hard numbers. Since the peak in employment in March 2001, the US economy has lost 2.4 million jobs. But that actually understates the jobs deficit. Historical averages for normal postrecession job growth indicate that employment should be some 8 million higher than it was in January. But estimates of outsourcing, while imprecise, are in the low- to mid-six figures, suggesting that it can explain no more than a twentieth of our jobs problem. And in a more "normal" economy, the US economy would generate half a million jobs every two months. Something else is clearly awry.

The most widely cited projections for offshoring come from Forrester Research, which estimated in a November 2002 report that 3.3 million service-industry jobs would go offshore by 2015. That looks like a big number, but it needs to be put in perspective. In January the United States had 108 million service jobs. According to the Bureau of Labor Statistics, the economy should add 22 million jobs between 2000 and 2010 (almost all of them in services); if we stretch that projection to account for the additional years in the Forrester study, that's 33 million. So the best estimates we have are that the outsourcing total equals about one in thirty of today's jobs, or one in ten of the next decade's new jobs.

> *Machines are doing more of the work, and people, less.*

Of course, these are headline-level statistics, aggregating sectors and occupations. Most of the job losses in the United States in recent years have not been in services, the main focus of offshoring worries, but in manufacturing. That sector has lost 3.3 million jobs over the past six years, or one in five—far more than during the early 1980s recession, the period that gave us the term Rust Belt.

Everyone knows where those went—Mexico first, then China, right? Maybe not. A study of twenty major economies done last fall by Joseph Carson, the chief economist at Alliance Capital, found that factory employment declined by 11 percent between 1995 and 2002. Brazil lost 20 percent of its manufacturing jobs, and China, rather stunningly, lost 15 percent (mainly because gains in the new private-sector enterprises weren't enough to offset losses in failing state enterprises). Factory employment rose in a handful of countries, but mostly by small amounts. The major reason for the shrinkage, Carson and other economists have explained, is the same as it's been for decades: Machines are doing more of the work, and people, less.

There once was a time when the service sector was expanding enough to offset losses in goods production. That hasn't been happening lately. Since the end of the recession, private service employment has expanded by just 619,000.

So what's up? We can never know for sure, but it's likely that this is what a postbubble economy looks like. After its bubble burst in 1989, Japan lived through more than a decade of economic stagnation, and it was years before people realized that the problem wasn't a matter of a short-term business cycle but something more profound. It's exaggerating only slightly to say that may be what a depression looks like in these days of big governments and indulgent central banks: no outright collapse, but no strong recovery either. But despite sustained low interest rates and bursts of public works spending, the Japanese economy just flatlined its way through the 1990s, and is only now showing signs of serious recovery.

Something similar may be happening here. Driven by exuberance and easy money, the bubble inspired firms to expand and hire aggressively; when the bust came, they were badly bruised. As a result, managers remain very wary about taking on new permanent staff. Worsening the problem is heavy pressure from Wall Street to get profits up; the easiest way to do that is to squeeze the existing work force harder. Almost every employed person you talk to has a tale of surviving workers' taking on the responsibilities of employees who leave voluntarily or are laid off. Pundits cite this as evidence of a continuing productivity miracle, but the reality of it is less glamorous—working harder and longer for no increase in pay. But it's much easier to look abroad for the source of our woes than it is to investigate the home-grown reasons.

Whatever the causes, though, our treatment of the unemployed and displaced is scandalously cruel. Fewer than half of the unemployed are drawing benefits. Public expenditure on retraining and job creation is risibly small. There's plenty that could and should be done here, from classic public works projects to less traditional ones like subsidized childcare. These should be the real issues; next to them, "offshoring" is a diversion.

A Mixed Result

By Terry Kosdrosky
Crain's Detroit Business, September 6, 2004

John James has seen the good and the bad created by the North American Free Trade Agreement.

On one hand, the chairman of Detroit-based James Group International Inc. lost a foreign trade-zone operation that employed 10 people at its peak. The trade zone—a place where imported goods can be assembled, repaired or destroyed before duties are paid—was rendered obsolete when NAFTA knocked down duties.

On the other hand, he established a new trucking partnership in 2001, Motor City Express, with Cambridge, Ontario-based Challenger Motor Freight. That operation thrives on cross-border shipping.

"While NAFTA might have put one of my companies out of business, it may have created an opportunity for another one," James said.

Ten years after it went into effect on Jan. 1, 1994, NAFTA created clear winners and losers—some within the same company—in metro Detroit. While proponents point to increased business with Canadian and Mexican partners and increased foreign investment in the area, opponents say that doesn't make up for the lost jobs or businesses who shrunk or closed.

Even NAFTA opponents agree it's been a boon for shareholders, owners, executives and middle-management employees at large companies such as multinational auto suppliers.

But ask owners of small or medium-sized businesses their opinion on NAFTA, and you'll get a range of opinions.

Grocers, shipping companies, auto suppliers and even some midsize toolmakers say NAFTA has helped their business. But small fabricators and injection molders have had a tough ride the past 10 years.

Squeezed by Cheaper Labor Costs

Brian Coons heard Ross Perot's famous "giant sucking sound" loud and clear. His Brico Fabricating & Welding Inc. lost contracts to Mexican and Canadian competitors that he said don't have nearly the wage and health insurance expenses carried by U.S. manufacturers.

Chesterfield Township-based Brico—a small shop that forms, welds and finishes small metal parts—is down to 16 employees, the smallest it's ever been, Coons said. He's had up to 22 employees working there. Those jobs pay in the $14-to-$16 an hour range with full health insurance.

Brico used to see profit margins of 12 percent to 15 percent. Now it's lucky to get 3 percent.

NAFTA squeezed Brico from the north and the south. Eliminating duties meant Mexican fabricators paying low wages could bid way below his profit margin. A duty-free North America meant Canadian companies could use their currency exchange rate to do the same.

Plus, neither Mexican nor Canadian companies pay $12,000 a month in health insurance premiums for 17 people, he said.

"NAFTA has drained us dramatically," Coons said. "Let's say I had an aluminum fabrication job, 100 pieces at $38 a piece. (A customer) can send it to Canada or Mexico and get 30 percent off." He said Brico has survived by having a specialty, aluminum components, and by producing flawless work.

Building New Infrastructure

But drive west along M-59 a bit and Fori Automation Inc. has a different story. The Shelby Township maker of assembly equipment says NAFTA is one of several reasons it's grown from between $40 million and $50 million in sales eight years ago to $80 million this year.

"We gained business in Canada and Mexico as our customers went there," said Paul Meloche, director of sales. "We have orders for $20 million worth of equipment to be delivered to Mexico in the next year and a half. It's built here and shipped there. We have the ability to drive our product to the site and not pay the high cost of taxes and duties."

Fori has acquired companies and opened plants in South Korea and Germany and has outsourced some basic work to Mexican companies. But employment here has grown from 140 to 190. The company manufactures chassis marriage systems, tire-and-wheel assembly machines and fluid-fill machines for assembly plants.

Meloche said Fori saw the world changing with NAFTA, the General Agreement on Tariffs and Trade and other free trade agreements. It helped that Fori had the means to expand overseas.

"Seven, eight years ago, we decided that we must be a global company, and we must compete with the Durrs and the Kukas of the world," Meloche said, referring to larger, European-based competitors.

Some Big Questions

NAFTA opponents say the gains for companies can't mask the fact that the trade agreement helped lead to the loss of manufacturing jobs in the area.

Free trade can be fair if agreements include minimum standards and protections for the inevitable losers. NAFTA had none of that, said David Bonior, former U.S. Representative from Macomb County. He was a vocal opponent of NAFTA, breaking with fellow Democrat President Clinton on the issue.

"As an example, before you joined the European Union, you had to meet certain standards," said Bonior, who is now teaching at Wayne State University in Detroit. "The Europeans put billions into their system so that individual counties can bring standards up to high levels, moving them upward. We didn't do that. It's free trade on the cheap."

Mexican environmental and workplace regulations didn't improve, giving Mexican businesses and farmers an unfair advantage over their U.S. counterparts. Mexican workers also didn't win the right to collectively bargain, dooming employees there to perpetual low

---

"We've created new jobs, but with fewer benefits and ones that are much less secure."
—**David Bonior, former U.S. Representative**

---

wages and keeping them an unfair threat to U.S. jobs. In fact, Bonior said Mexican workers are making about the same now, as adjusted for inflation, as they were 10 years ago.

That's not what Bill Barrett, president and CEO of Taylor-based Trans-Man Logistics Inc., sees. He said the Mexican government has improved its business climate greatly. Trans-Man manages cross-border shipping throughout North America.

Barrett said Mexico changed its customs services to match U.S. and Canadian standards. Corruption is much less rampant and business regulations also are more uniform, he said.

"If anything, NAFTA has enhanced Mexican standards to the point where it's upgraded to standards equal to the U.S. and Canada," Barrett said.

For workers, Bonior said, NAFTA has been a "disaster."

"In the United States, particularly in Michigan, we've seen good-paying jobs leave to go to Mexico and, now, China because of these neo-liberal trade regimes," Bonior said. "We've created new jobs, but with fewer benefits and ones that are much less secure."

As of July, federal unemployment numbers show Michigan has about 686,000 manufacturing jobs, the lowest number since 1990.

How much of that is due to NAFTA is difficult to pinpoint. The U.S. Labor Department said the United States lost 507,358 jobs from October 1993 to September 2002 due to NAFTA, according to

Knight Ridder News Service. The U.S. economy created about 200,000 jobs a month during that time. The department stopped reporting NAFTA-related job losses in 2002.

Interest groups report varying NAFTA-related job numbers.

A Complex Situation

But NAFTA's true negative effects aren't just felt in job losses, said Donald Boggs, president of the Metropolitan Detroit AFL-CIO. Local economies suffer when employment shifts from manufacturing jobs to service jobs, he said. Salaries go down and service jobs typically don't carry the medical and pension benefits manufacturing jobs offer, he said. About 22 percent of factory workers who lose their jobs wind up in the service industry, Boggs said.

"We will see the impact of NAFTA 20 years from now when everybody has to go on Social Security without health care," he said.

But other good-paying jobs are created, proponents say. Foreign investment in metro Detroit boomed after NAFTA. In 1992, 579

"Whether we like it or not, everybody in America doesn't go to college and pick up a skilled trade." —**Donald Boggs, president, Metro Detroit AFL-CIO**

---

foreign-owned companies set up shop in the area, according to the Detroit Regional Chamber. Now there are 849. Foreign-owned suppliers such as Behr North America Inc. have spent millions on R&D centers and headquarters in metro Detroit.

While not all are due to NAFTA, it's clear foreign companies didn't want to miss out on serving a three-country market. For an automotive-related company, Detroit makes a natural base, said John Carroll, vice president for business development for the chamber.

A recent study commissioned by the chamber also found that manufacturing job losses in the last three years were mostly due to productivity and technology improvements. About 12.5 percent of jobs lost from 2000 to 2003 were due to moving jobs offshore or importing more foreign-made goods, according to the study by the Troy-based Accelerator Group L.L.C. The study also noted that laid-off manufacturing workers find jobs that pay an average of 67 percent of their former salary.

The AFL-CIO's Boggs said the new jobs created aren't the kind that a person with a high-school education can obtain so they can raise a family.

"Whether we like it or not, everybody in America doesn't go to college and pick up a skilled trade," he said. "You have to have some kind of mechanism for somebody to leave high school and making a living for a family."

Benefits for Consumers

But NAFTA has other, hard-to-see benefits for working people, said Jamal Koussan, co-owner of Super Greenland Grocery Inc. in Dearborn. NAFTA eliminated tariffs and quotas on all but a handful of agricultural goods. Greenland imports poultry, cooking oil and produce, especially seedless cucumbers, from Canada.

That results in lower prices for consumers and helps Greenland. Low prices bring more shoppers to the store and they spend more, Koussan said.

"This is something that, as an American business, helped me quite a bit," he said. "It was good for all involved, us and the consumer."

To underscore the point, Greenland's prices increased recently as agricultural trade between the United States and Canada has taken a hit due to a case of mad cow disease in Canada and a general cooling of relations between the two countries.

Greenland customers have noticed, as produce once shipped cheaply from Canada now comes from Arizona or California with extra shipping costs. The cucumbers alone cost an extra $5 a box to ship from Arizona, Koussan said.

"We can't run the specials we used to," he said.

While Canada's farms might benefit people in Detroit, its strong plastics industry had hurt local plastics companies and workers. When duties were eliminated, the weak Canadian dollar made it difficult to compete, said Jan Roncelli, president of Troy-based Bermar Associates Inc.

Bermar faced a flood of bids from Canada that were much lower than anything a U.S. company could match. Two years ago, Bermar lost a bid on job to a competitor that had a plant in Mexico. Bermar's customers are mostly machine builders.

"We were getting underbid by 25 to 40 percent," Roncelli said. "We lost jobs because we could not compete. That's into the profit margin. U.S. manufacturers don't reap the benefits of free trade."

Bermar has survived by selling its service and design capabilities. Still, it's a bigger struggle than it used to be, Roncelli said.

"We haven't entered into the nonprofit realm yet, but some days I have no eraser left on my pencil," she said.

While that's the case at some small manufacturers, others might not be in business but for NAFTA. Dearborn-based Amerigon Inc. relied on NAFTA as part of its business model.

Amerigon makes small electrical devices that heat and cool automotive seats. It employs 10 in Dearborn and 40 at an R&D center in California. But its manufacturing is done in Mexico. It's a growing company—revenue jumped from $15.3 million in 2002 to $29 million in 2003—that needed the low labor rates in Mexico to get automakers to accept the product.

CEO Dan Coker said Amerigon was asking automakers to add a new component at a time of massive cost-cutting.

"We do have a new item and we were asking them to take a leap with us," he said. "(NAFTA) has been a very key part of our business model. It was very critical for us to be cost competitive."

James Group International's James, who both won and lost business because of NAFTA, said businesses need to move on when events they can't control affect the bottom line.

"I'm not going around complaining NAFTA put me out of business," he said. "I just started looking elsewhere."

IV. The Working World in Transition

Editor's Introduction

Of all the ends met by armed Americans in the current conflict in Iraq, perhaps the most shocking came on March 31, 2004, when a group of Iraqis in the city of Fallujah killed and mutilated four men—Wesley Batalona, Stephen Helvenston, Mike Teague, and Jerko Zovko—who were part of a small convoy passing through the city. Though all four men were experienced and well-trained veterans—Helvenston was a former Navy SEAL, the others one-time members of Army Ranger units—and were assigned to protect a shipment of materiel destined for U.S. forces, none of them were members of the military. Instead, they worked for Blackwater USA, one of a new breed of private companies that specialize in providing services to the armed forces that until recently would have been administered directly. In that sense, what happened to these men—and the more than 400 other private contractors who have died in Iraq since the conflict began—is a detail in the still-unfolding history of the privatization of government services that began in the 1980s and continues to this day.

Yet the story of Batalona, Helvenston, Teague, and Zovko is also about America's newly flexible workforce. Helveston, for example, went from the Navy to making exercise videos, consulting on movies, and performing in reality television shows before taking a short-term contract with Blackwater. In other words, after gaining a certain broad base of skills, he parlayed them into a series of varied work situations, choosing his jobs in much the same way that some people choose where to live.

The first four articles in this chapter address different facets of this new emphasis on worker flexibility—albeit on a more day-to-day level. "Critics Wary of Benefits Permatemps Miss Out On," by Maria M. Perotin, introduces perhaps the most flexible of all workers: the temporary employee, or temp, who may spend years working without ever gaining a permanent position. In "Temp-to-Hire Is Becoming Full-Time Practice at Firms," John Zappe explores the increasing tendency among companies to offer jobs on a temporary basis before converting them into more traditionally defined positions.

Retirees are another group of Americans who approach their working lives with an eye toward flexibility. In her wide-ranging selection "Heaven Can Wait," Paula Span details the current array of options available to many Americans in their 60s and 70s, while also anticipating where today's trends are likely to lead for the next generation. Span expects the age at which people achieve full retirement to be pushed ever higher and that some workers will slowly ease into retirement, as part of a shift toward what is called phased retirement. Telecommuting is another method by which workers and employers can achieve optimum flexibility, but, as Roger Fillion makes clear in

"Doing Homework," telecommuting can also provide jobs for people who might otherwise be unemployed, such as the quadriplegic man Fillion describes at the beginning of his article.

In "Phased Retirement Keeps Employees—and Keeps Them Happy," Sarah Fister Gale looks at how some businesses and universities are using phased retirement as a way of retaining the special skills and knowledge of older workers. The strategy is also used as a defensive business technique. "These people want to continue working, even if they have to create their own opportunities," Gale quotes one expert as saying. "If you don't have a phased-retirement plan, they may be taking their talents to the competition."

The final two entries in this section highlight another important workplace trend: the use of technology by employers to screen applicants and monitor current workers. Karen Dybis, in "Firms Go High-Tech to Screen Applicants," describes the use of detailed background checks—including inquiries into a potential hire's credit history—by some firms in order to assess the suitability of an applicant. The scrutiny companies apply to potential hires can also be carried over to the people already working for them. Patricia Kitchen, in "Yes, the Boss Is . . .Watching," reviews some of the methods—and rationales—now used for monitoring employees and anticipates even more technologically advanced measures that may be initiated in the future, such as implanting radio frequency identification chips under the skin, to identify and track workers as they do their jobs.

Critics Wary of Benefits Permatemps Miss Out On

By Maria M. Perotin
Fort Worth Star-Telegram, July 24, 2002

Once in a while, Kay Collings lands an office job that brings steady paychecks for several months.

More often, the temporary worker from Bedford, Texas, has to settle for a fraction of the money, erratic schedules and hot days driving an airport jetbridge.

After her 23-year career at Sabre Holdings ended with a layoff in 1999, Collings joined the legion of temps who now work in virtually all U.S. industries.

They are the clerks and machine operators who work for a few weeks in an office or factory. The laborers who toil a day at a time at construction sites. The technology whizzes whose jobs last only as long as their current upgrade project.

All told, 12.5 million U.S. workers—about 9.2 percent of the labor force—now have such "alternative employment arrangements," according to the U.S. Bureau of Labor Statistics. It doesn't stop there: Government projections call for temporary staffing companies to grow 49 percent by 2010—adding 1.9 million new jobs, more than any other industry.

Temps were among the first to lose jobs in the current economic downturn, and they're expected to be first to benefit from a recovery as employers slowly rebuild their staffs.

For U.S. businesses, the sometimes-employees represent an agile labor force, with low costs and inherent flexibility. But critics of the temp explosion worry that it's forcing workers into dead-end employment where they're often shut out from health insurance, retirement benefits and paid time off.

Collings hasn't received such perks from an employer in years. Her only benefit as a temp: A Fort Worth, Texas, company where she worked for six months picked up her downtown parking tab.

More recently, she has spent 12 months working off-and-on, part-time, for a charter airline. Some days, she staffs a ticket counter and others a jetbridge.

She's only called when she's needed, and she's paid by the flight. So a typical workday can include a three-hour shift starting at 5 a.m. followed by another spurt of duties in midafternoon.

The experiences, as well as previous temporary stints, have been eye-opening for Collings.

"You kind of feel like a third foot, because you're not really part of the office force," Collings said. "You're an object, not a person. You are the temp, and you're kind of faceless and voiceless."

The dearth of benefits troubles labor advocates, who complain that employers cut costs by treating temporary workers—even those who work for long stretches of time—differently than their permanent counterparts.

Although temporary workers have the same legal rights as full-fledged staffers, such as minimum wage and job safety protections, companies can save big dollars by denying them benefits, said Catherine Ruckelshaus, a director of the National Employment Law Project's Subcontracted Worker Initiative. Classifying workers as "independent contractors" instead of employees can trim corporate tax bills, too.

The temp industry has surged in recent years, reaching an average of 2.18 million workers daily [in 2001].

As an example, Ruckelshaus cites the "permatemps" who reached a $97 million legal settlement with Microsoft in 2000.

Those workers filed suit in 1992, challenging a practice that effectively created a two-tier system of employees and classified some as temporary for as long as 14 years.

"The permanents got stock options and benefits, and the temps didn't," she said.

Temp workers generally qualify for benefits if they join a staffing company for a length of time, said Richard Wahlquist, president of the American Staffing Association. But many don't stick around that long because they regard temp jobs as a pit stop on the road to permanent employment.

"Seventy-five percent of the folks that come to staffing companies hope that they're going to be there for a period of time and then transition," Wahlquist said.

On average, temp companies' workers spend 11 weeks on various assignments, and the work force turns over 400 percent a year, he said.

The temp industry has surged in recent years, reaching an average of 2.18 million workers daily last year. That's more than double the temp agencies' employment in 1990, but it's down from a peak of 2.54 million daily workers in 2000.

Now, after a 17-month period of declining employment, orders for temp workers have improved in each of the past four months, Wahlquist said.

Much of the industry's growth has come at Manpower Inc., the Milwaukee-based industry leader that employs 2 million people worldwide annually.

Kathi Fleck, a Grand Prairie, Texas–based area manager for Manpower, said the most significant transformation has come not in the larger size of the temporary work force but in its infiltration into every area of business. Companies that once relied on temps only to fill in for vacationing secretaries now use agencies to hire all manner of workers.

"We used to be unloading trucks and sweeping a floor, vs. being a part of their distribution center now," she said.

The bulk of employers hire temp workers for long-term assignments, Fleck said. Some use Manpower's service to check out workers' performance before offering them permanent jobs.

Tim Costello, coordinator of the North American Alliance for Fair Employment, said the spread of temporary labor is eliminating job security not only for the temps but also for permanent workers who fear they could be replaced.

His 6-year-old group wants regulations that would require employers to offer the same pay and benefits to all workers—permanent, temporary, full-time and part-time.

> *"The temporary help angle helps employers to control some of the swings."*
> —Tom Dilworth, Employment Policies Institute

"There's been a gradual shift to contingent staffing strategies," Costello said. "It's going to lead to lower wages, poorer working conditions and more instability, which is perhaps even more important."

Those fears are wildly overblown, the Employment Policies Institute says.

Millions of workers opt for temporary employment by choice, and they often rely on the experience to obtain new skills before moving on to better jobs, said Tom Dilworth, research director at the business-backed think tank.

"Some of them are using it as a temporary-to-permanent type of opportunity. Some of them want to get a foot in the door. Some of them only have a limited amount of time to work," Dilworth said. "A lot of employees want that flexibility."

For businesses, that flexibility can mean the difference between survival and ruin, he said.

Many employers wouldn't be able to turn a profit if they couldn't expand and shrink their roster as demand fluctuates, he said. For example, amusement parks need more workers in the warm months when they're swamped with vacationers. And some factories must run round-the-clock for part of the year, but then slow down dramatically at other times.

Temporary workers are also a buffer during economic downturns, he said. Employers can cut them loose as business drops off, and then add temps quickly when orders start trickling in.

"The temporary help angle helps employers to control some of the swings," Dilworth said.

Southlake, Texas, resident Stacey Hamaker made the choice to give up permanent work more than a decade ago.

The systems analyst works one contract at a time, sometimes spending months between jobs for various clients.

"It's my preference, because I have children and it gives me more flexibility," she said. "In the long run, I've been happy."

Nonetheless, the economy's current funk has made contracts so scarce that Hamaker is rethinking her independence.

"The good news is you can work when you want, but the bad news is you can't always get work when you want," she said.

Like Hamaker, the vast majority of independent contractors preferred their arrangements to joining employers' payrolls, according to the Bureau of Labor Statistics. But more than half of "contingent workers"—all those who report that their jobs are temporary—say they would favor permanent jobs.

Among contingent workers, median weekly earnings were $432 when the agency last inquired in February 2001. Only about a fifth received employer-provided insurance coverage or pension benefits.

Camilo Munoz, a Grapevine, Texas, information technology worker who contracts his services, said he would love a regular job. But permanent posts are few and far between in his field.

"I'm an old-fashioned, conservative kind of person when it comes to work," Munoz said. "I like better full-time positions. It doesn't give you any security, but it gives you a little more stability."

Without a steady job, Munoz relies for income on whatever contract he can nab—some lasting a full year and others for only one month. "I'll take it, because it's a month," he said. "At least it's going to help."

Collings understands that pragmatism.

"Anything is better than nothing right now. In today's economy, I think you're fortunate if you find a temp job," she said. "There's a lot of people that aren't even doing temp stuff."

Temp-to-Hire Is Becoming Full-Time Practice at Firms

By John Zappe
Workforce Management, June 1, 2005

Last fall, when T-Mobile needed hundreds of engineers and technicians for the new cell system it acquired from a competitor, the company went straight to its staffing vendors. Other than perhaps for the numbers, it was a routine procurement. There was one exception, however: T-Mobile took the opportunity to include a temp-to-hire clause in the contract.

"It's not been a regular course of business in the past," says John Sullivan, T-Mobile area director of engineering and operations for Northern California. He supervises some 250 employees, of whom about 110 are contingent workers. Of the company's 22,000 employees nationwide, 20 percent to 30 percent are contingent.

"Many of them are not necessarily interested in full-time work," he says. "But for those who are, it's a chance for us to see who's a fit and it gives them the chance to see this is a pretty good place."

T-Mobile didn't set out to use the temporary engagements as a tryout period; it didn't intend to use the staffing vendors as a sort of outsourced recruiter. But when the opportunity arose, the company figured, "Why not?" Sullivan says.

"Why not?" increasingly appears to be a question being asked by companies already comfortable with hiring temporary workers. Whether they turned to contingent workers because of a sudden upturn in business and then developed a strategy around the need or they strategically decided to build a flexible workforce before hiring their first temp, these companies are finding hidden values in what was once regarded as second-class staff.

It's a hiring tactic and not a workforce strategy, says Simon Billsberry, CEO of Kineticom, a staffing contractor in San Diego. But "as a tactic it's very beneficial. We're seeing it more. There is significant growth in the temp-to-perm area."

"Try before you buy" is becoming quite popular in some areas, Billsberry adds-so much so that the largest of the companies with flexible workforces have been pushing staffing contractors to cut or even eliminate the conversion fees they have to pay when hiring a contingent worker.

Losing an office temp to a client has long been a fact of life for companies like Kelly, Manpower and AppleOne. They and other staffing contractors try to limit the practice by assessing fees sometimes exceeding 30 percent of a year's salary to the hiring company. But finding office workers is a snap compared to hiring an engineer with specialized skills in a growth area. To staffing companies, such employees are a revenue-making asset that they don't want to have to keep replacing if they can avoid it. Increasingly, though, they can't.

> *"There is a war for talent. We compete for the best people with everyone else."*
> —Simon Billsberry, CEO, Kineticom

Gary Noke, president of Decision Logic, a division of TAC Worldwide Cos., says that after one of his company's workers has been on a client job for six months, the client can hire the worker without a fee. "The larger companies are forcing that on the contractors," Noke says. With larger companies, that fee-free conversion provision is always required, he says.

Contractor As Recruiter

With the iffy economic recovery, companies that in another time would have ramped up their full-time staff are hiring contingent workers with a conversion right. Once they become convinced that the business uptick isn't just a temporary spike, they'll look first to the temporary workers to fill vacancies.

"Your contractor," Noke says, "becomes your recruiter."

Staffing companies uniformly grumble about that: They do the recruiting, while the client gets to pick over the staff and hire away the best of the workers.

"There is a war for talent," says Billsberry, whose company—like all the staffing contractors—recruits year round. "We compete for the best people with everyone else. It's in my best interest to keep them working because they'll go somewhere else." It's a competition among two or three other staffing companies to find talent and keep them working with Kineticom's clients, he says.

The only ace for the contractors is that many of the most in-demand workers prefer short-term assignments and would rather not work for a single company.

That's long been the case for IT workers and certain types of engineers who naturally fit into project work. When the project ends, they move on to another—sometimes with the same company, but often not. At the end of the 20th century, with the specter of wholesale computer failures looming, thousands of programmers came out of retirement and academia and even left regular jobs to take on high-paying Y2K projects. In January 2001, they retired again or signed on with staffing contractors for project work rather than go back to full-time cubicle life.

T-Mobile's Sullivan says that even though he has a fee-free conversion right, he believes that most of his contingent workers aren't interested in becoming employees. There are cultural issues—many of his techs are noncitizens—that might prevent it. The pay differential is higher for a temp and, Sullivan says, "some people just like to be able to do something different."

Hiring contingent workers was once a matter of necessity to help a company get through a busy cycle. And working as a temp was a matter of survival, a way to earn some money until the next "real" job came along.

That's still the case and, say recruiters and staffing contractors, likely always will be.

Mellon Bank, for instance, was ramping up for a special credit card offer and needed hundreds of short-term workers at its call center in New Jersey. Greg Antonelle, recruiting director for Aim-Hire Associates, helped fill the bank's need. As the campaign winds down, the temp staff will too.

But with the changing nature of the economy and with highly skilled IT workers blazing the trail over the past two decades, building a flexible workforce has become a strategy and not just a tactic. Adding contingent workers to the workforce mix is an accepted way of doing business not only at the Fortune 500 level, but increasingly for medium-sized businesses as well.

A strategically hired contingent workforce can be even more productive than full-time staff, says Chris Hagler, national director of strategic services for Resources Global Professional. "They don't get involved in company politics," Hagler says. "They are not wrapped up in all the things you find staff talking about at the water cooler. They come in and do their job."

Hiring to Fit Unique Needs

Companies make a strategic workforce decision by sizing up their cyclical needs, workforce costs, time to hire, core functions and even image. Looking at each of these components and deciding both their value and how they can best be managed will lead to developing a workforce strategy that might include a mix of full- and part-time employees, contingent workers and outsourced work.

Hagler, who helps companies work through these issues, offers an example. For Coca-Cola, marketing is a core function, but accounts receivable is not, she says. And so the company keeps its marketing operation in-house, with full-time staff, and outsources the accounting function. For a bottler, the decision might be to have only a minimum number of line workers and supplement them with temps to handle sudden demand.

"If you have a really strategic HR person, they will look at what is core and what is not. They'll work with the other divisions to assess demand and need and develop an overall strategy that creates a flexible workforce," Hagler says.

Her company, like many of its rivals, specializes in placing professional talent including accountants, chief information officers, supply-chain specialists and HR experts. Resources Global Professional recently began to provide lawyers on a temporary basis.

American Staffing Association data attest to the strength of the temp market. The ASA reported that last year nearly 2.5 million people on average were working as contract and temporary employees every day, the highest level since the go-go days of 2000. That was almost 2 percent of the nation's total nonfarm workforce. To keep that many people working, staffing firms had to recruit and hire 11.7 million employees during the year.

The ASA estimates that 8 million of them transitioned to full-time work during the year, but not necessarily with their client's company. However, an ASA survey found that conversion fees paid to staffing companies for hiring away their workers came to $7.3 billion last year, which represents almost 10 percent of total revenue for the staffing industry.

Analysts project that the staffing industry will see even greater growth this year, not only because of organic economic growth but because large companies are embracing the concept.

"The companies that get it are moving to have a permanent flexible workforce," Noke says. "And most of the bigger companies get it."

One of those companies is Johnson & Johnson.

Olivia Baumgartner, a recruiter with Johnson & Johnson Professional Recruiting, the company's internal hiring arm, says contingent workers are a key part of the company's workforce. Indeed, about half the 90 employees in her office are temporary consultants. "We just grew so fast," she says.

Baumgartner has worked in human resources for several companies, including a recent stint as a manager at Hewlett-Packard, and says she has seen contingent staffing become a way of life.

"It's cost-effective and it gives a company a chance to look over the workers and try and buy," she says. Workers like it too, Baumgartner adds. "They get a chance to learn about a company and get a broad exposure to the different ways companies do things."

She should know. At HP and now at Johnson & Johnson, Baumgartner is part of the contingent staff.

Heaven Can Wait

By Paula Span
The Washington Post, September 11, 2005

There are things about his job that Jim Martin doesn't love, like getting up at 5:25 each morning so he can squeeze in a workout at the gym before eating breakfast en route to work. Or the trafficky hour-long drive from his Manassas condo to his Annandale office, and the same lousy drive back. By the time he slogs home, fixes himself a martini and has dinner with his wife, there's not much time left for all the other things he'd like to be doing—learning Spanish, for instance, or painting with watercolors. People at his stage of life are supposed to be able to indulge such interests.

But any gripes are outweighed by the things he does appreciate about his job developing spreadsheets and tracking income for the Purple Heart Foundation. There's the salary that buttresses an upper-middle-class life he's loath to give up, of course, but he also values the liveliness, the stimulation, the feeling of contributing to an honorable endeavor. In particular, he cherishes his small cadre of co-workers at the organization, which provides services for veterans and their families. "I love these people like children," he says one morning, settling in at his computer. "And some of them are young enough to be my children."

A few days ago, the staff put together a lunch to celebrate his birthday. His colleague across the hall picked up sandwiches; someone brought balloons (one is still wilting in Martin's office); someone else contributed a key lime pie with a single candle. Everyone sang, then presented Martin with a card signed with affectionate insults, which he's tacked to his bulletin board. "With age comes wisdom," one colleague wrote. "You must be VERY wise."

He is 71, a joke-teller and raconteur with a broad, ruddy face, a remarkable amount of wavy silver hair and empathic gray-green eyes. His endocrinologist regularly thwacks him in the midsection and says, "You've gotta lose that," but he actually looks fine, fit and healthy.

It's something of an illusion. "I have two diseases that will kill me one day; it's a matter of when," Martin likes to say, cheerfully. He's diabetic, and there's a pocket sewn inside the flowered Hawaiian shirt he's worn to work this morning to hold an insulin pump. Later in the morning, he unzips a small black kit, as he does four times each day, wipes his fingertip with an alcohol swab and tests his blood sugar. "Ooh, 216, very high, very high," he mutters, checking the meter, then using the pump to administer additional insulin.

Having lived for years with diabetes—along with high blood pressure and, more recently, coronary artery disease—Martin found it perhaps less frightening than it otherwise might have been to be seated across from an oncologist last winter. The doctor was so intent on shuffling papers, never quite meeting his eyes, that Martin braced for bad news, and he got it: "Mr. Martin, I have to tell you that you have leukemia." But it was chronic lymphocytic leukemia, a very slow form, the oncologist went on to say. One of Martin's other illnesses—this was evidently the good news—would probably kill him first.

So, having assessed the personal and financial costs and benefits, in the way that 45 years as a manager and consultant trained him to do, Martin is still happy to come to the office each day. After his birthday lunch, he thanked the singers, cautioned, "Don't go on the nightclub circuit just yet," and went back to work.

The experts have come to a strikingly widespread consensus: Never mind that golden-years stuff. Keep working.

Which makes him at once an unusual figure—only about 14 percent of those over 65 remain in the labor force—and a potential role model. A massing alliance of researchers and analysts, lobbyists and advocates, opinion leaders, wonks of all sorts, would likely applaud him, because Martin's doing just what they wish the rest of us would do. Having examined the demographic trends, the labor force stats, the health and longevity data, the projected costs of Social Security, Medicare and other government programs, the experts have come to a strikingly widespread consensus: Never mind that golden-years stuff. Keep working.

Not forever; no one's proposing to abolish retirement. But after many decades in which people embarked on retirement at younger and younger ages, we're now being urged to delay it, possibly by quite a few years.

Forget that dot-com-era idea of cashing out at 55, the wonks advise. Let 62, Social Security's "early" retirement age, pass, and its "full" retirement ages, too. Seventy is the new 65.

At the heart of this proposed change is a fundamental mismatch: We are living longer, remaining healthy longer. We're better educated, less likely to have labored in coal mines and steel plants that cripple or deplete us. Thus, we're much better able than our forebears to remain in the workforce—but we're not doing it. We're bailing out, most of us, as soon as we possibly can.

The idea of contemporary retirement, a phase of life that caps decades of work with years of freedom and leisure, has become so ingrained, so pervasive, that we forget how recent an invention it really is. It's younger than Jim Martin.

The major exodus from work began after World War II. Social Security first paid benefits in 1940, expanded to include more workers through the '50s, was bolstered by Medicare in the '60s (when that early retirement option also appeared) and was further strengthened in the '70s, when Congress built in annual cost-of-living increases. Like the private pension plans also proliferating during this period, Social Security was meant to protect those who'd grown too ill or frail to continue working, but also to encourage older employees to yield to the incoming tide of youth.

It worked amazingly well: A graph depicting older workers' participation in the labor market over the past half-century resembles a ski slope. Nearly half of American men over 65 were in the workforce in 1950; by 1985, fewer than 16 percent had or were seeking jobs. The proportion of men age 55 to 64 in the labor force has fallen sharply as well. Most workers now retire in their early sixties—because they can.

But also because retirement has become increasingly attractive. Greater wealth means that most retirees no longer need to move in with their children, but can live independently. Technology, as MIT economist Dora Costa points out in her influential book *The Evolution of Retirement*, has provided lots of affordable new forms of recreation, from RVs to TVs to PCs. Marketers, bent on persuading retirees to buy vitamins and Sun Belt condos, have created the now-familiar image of that silver-haired couple who spend so much time dancing on beaches and cruise ships.

"It's come to be an expected part of the life course," says David Ekerdt, director of the gerontology center at the University of Kansas. "We're encouraged to want it, plan for it, yearn for it. It's the new ending of the American dream."

Oops.

Vastly increased longevity isn't really a crisis; it's one of humanity's great accomplishments. That a man who retires at 62 will now survive long enough to receive Social Security benefits for an average 17 years, a woman for 20 years—this is good news.

But how to finance all those additional years, with the largest generation in the nation's history about to retire? Starting in two years, the first of 78 million baby boomers will turn 62 and begin applying for Social Security benefits, then become eligible for Medicare three years later. FDR, and the other governmental architects of retirement, didn't anticipate this.

In May, economist Eugene Steuerle, part of a squadron of retirement researchers at the Urban Institute and a boomer himself at 58, warned a congressional committee that his generation's legacy might be "to bequeath a government whose almost sole purpose is to finance our own consumption in retirement." Steuerle, a leading alarm-sounder about such issues, predicts that tens of millions of additional early retirees could not only bankrupt the programs meant to underwrite their retirement but also soak up so much of the federal budget that there's virtually nothing left for any other purpose.

Moreover, after the boom comes the baby bust, the sharply smaller group born between 1965 and 1976. It's not only too small to support all the retired boomers, it's too small to fill all the jobs a healthy economy will require. For the first time in decades, analysts are worried about a labor shortage—of about 10 million workers by the end of this decade.

So one prescription is obvious. Whatever else lawmakers do or don't do—if they raise the age of Social Security or Medicare eligibility, if they establish private retirement accounts, if they index benefits for longevity—it would be a fine thing, the wonks agree, if we'd keep working.

"The biggest financial decision most people make is when to retire."
—Eugene Steuerle, researcher, Urban Institute

It's practically the public-spirited thing to do. If we remained in the workforce longer—and labor force participation among older workers does appear to be inching upward—we could postpone the age at which we receive Social Security checks, thus easing the drain. The higher taxes we would keep paying (including continued Social Security contributions) would help fill the federal coffers. And we could ward off a labor shortage that might threaten the whole economy.

We'd reap personal benefits, too, the keep-working partisans argue. "The biggest financial decision most people make is when to retire," Steuerle says. "It's far more important than whether they put their money in stocks or bonds." Most retirees, he points out, have few such private assets; they're mainly dependent on government. And in terms of Social Security benefits, "just working one more year often gives people a good 6 to 10 percent more income every year after that."

Maybe we'd even enjoy those senior years more, since studies show that retirees engaged in "productive" activities—including paid work—are more satisfied than the unengaged.

Delaying retirement, however, requires serious changes, some of them distinctly unpopular. It means, among other things:

(a) Modifying traditional pension practices and regulations that discourage people from working longer.

(b) Persuading employers to get as excited about retaining or hiring older workers as labor analysts are.

And (c) subjecting the societal expectations and sense of entitlement built up over 70 years to a fast U-turn.

The last one could be the hard part. After urging sixtysomething workers to relax and withdraw, to look forward to days without time clocks, to dance and play golf and volunteer and flee winter without guilt because they'd earned these years of income-without-work, America proposes to add a loud "Not yet!"

A few friends are coming over for a barbecue this evening, so Jim and Anna Martin hit the Old Town farmer's market this morning and picked up fresh produce and a raspberry pie. Now Anna is flitting around the kitchen making deviled eggs, while Jim—aka "the grillmeister"—attends to an important matter in their home office.

He's assembling several copies of a durable power of attorney (for Virginia) and a designation of health care surrogate (required in Florida, where Anna's mother left her a small prefab house they visit once or twice a year). "That little girl in Florida got us thinking," Jim says, referring to the late Terry Schiavo, who hadn't put her end-of-life wishes in writing. He and Anna now have, and he's folding a set of signed documents into an envelope for his son, Jeffery, in Little Rock, Ark. "We put one in the safe-deposit box, we have one here in the house, and we're sending one to him."

Task accomplished, he joins Anna in the kitchen; it's once more time to test his blood sugar. "One twenty-seven," he says. "A little high, but not bad, not bad at all."

He keeps his diabetes under control, Jim says with some pride. But managing that, and his other health problems, requires unrelenting effort, involving not only frequent doctors' visits but "every pill known to Western medicine." One of the cabinets holds a thicket of little bottles: For the hypertension he's had for 30 years, an ACE inhibitor and a drug to lower triglycerides. For the coronary artery disease, a beta blocker, a blood thinner and a cholesterol-reducer. Pills to treat acid reflux and nerve pain from his diabetes. Plus various herbal medicines and a host of vitamins and minerals.

Ten years ago, Jim had an angioplasty to reopen a blocked artery. "I haven't had any more problems with it," says Jim, whose discussions of this stuff tend to be matter of fact, even comical. "But whenever you get a pain anywhere in your upper body, you think, 'Uh oh, this is it . . . goodbye, cruel world.'" And there is pain. Five years ago, he had surgery to fuse several vertebrae in his neck. His diabetes makes simply walking painful most of the time, though he chooses not to dwell on that.

Under the circumstances, it's not surprising that his wife and his two children, from an earlier marriage, express mixed feelings about Jim's continuing to work. Anna, a decade younger and still teaching orchestral music in the Prince William County public schools, is in favor. "Business has been his life," she says. "It makes him feel functional." His son concurs. But his daughter, Laura, in Lafayette, Ind., isn't so sanguine. "He's worked long enough and hard enough," she argues. "People, when they get to retirement age, should be able to retire."

Martin has indeed worked hard, ever since he graduated from high school in Attica, Ind., a two-traffic-light factory town, in 1952. His family couldn't afford to send him to school, so he spent three years in the Army, then entered Purdue University on the GI Bill, earning a physics degree and a master's in industrial administration.

Once he'd graduated, Martin spent nearly two decades managing manufacturing plants, first an Indiana factory that produced retail display fixtures, then an office equipment maker in North Carolina. For the second half of his career—though it may turn out to be the middle third—he was a management and training consultant with such clients as U.S. Steel, Clairol, Philips Lighting and several big pharmaceutical houses. During much of that time he was such a road warrior, leaving home on Sunday afternoons and not returning until Friday evenings, that when Anna received a tempting job offer in 1989, the thought of relocating from North Carolina to Virginia barely fazed him. "As long as there's an airport," he told her, and they moved.

Partway through his sixties, though, he began to sense a change. "Most of the mid-management people you work with are in their forties to mid-fifties," Martin says. "They don't want to hire old guys . . . I could discern what was coming down the road." And the travel was wearing him out. He started looking for "a real job, where you go to the same office every day." The director of Senior Employment Resources in Annandale, where he'd volunteered to teach a weekly computer class for older workers, told him the Purple Heart Foundation needed a part-time consultant.

"Jim's a great asset," says the foundation's executive director, Dick Gallant. "I discuss things with him. If you have a problem, he can bring in multiple years of experience." Initially, Martin warded off Gallant's offers of full-time employment; he liked having long weekends and besides, the salary wasn't high enough. Then three years ago, Gallant upped the offer, and it was.

The money matters. Martin acknowledges that he could retire right now—on his $1,200 a month from Social Security, a small pension from the Indiana plant and personal savings—but he couldn't live in this rambling new 2,300-square-foot condo with a gas fireplace and an oversize bathtub and two decks under construction. (A ceramic plaque in the bedroom reads: "Do Not Resist Growing Old— Many Are Denied the Privilege.") Purchased for about $320,000 two years ago, it's not cheaper than the house they sold at the other end of town, but it's easier to let someone else worry about the yardwork and maintenance.

He could retire—but he probably couldn't afford to accompany Anna and her students to music festivals in Europe each spring. The Martins have visited England and Scotland and next year are planning their fourth trip to Maastricht in the Netherlands. Their season tickets to the National Symphony Orchestra, and those gracious restaurant meals before the concerts, might have to go. Eating out in general would have to be trimmed back.

"We're working because we want this lifestyle," Jim explains. "And we'd have to change it if we stopped. We'd have to move someplace less expensive, or I'd have to win the lottery." But he doesn't buy lottery tickets. And Anna plans to work for several years—she likes teaching and also wants to fatten her pension—so that rules out, for now, decamping for North Carolina or another low-cost location. Plus, there was that grim period five years ago when Jim's love of technology, and tech stocks, meant that each monthly brokerage statement looked scarier than the last. "You'd keep watching that bottom number go down and down and down, and you'd say, 'Is it ever going to end?'" He estimates he lost about $150,000 in paper profits.

> *"We're working because we want this lifestyle."*
> —**Jim Martin, Purple Heart Foundation**

So his job, which pays something more than $40,000 a year, makes the difference between getting by okay and enjoying the standard of living he and Anna are accustomed to. Happily, it also meets Jim's personal criterion for enjoyable work, which is that you don't dread Sunday nights.

"The only thing I don't like about it," he says, "is the same thing I wouldn't like about any job: the lack of freedom, the time to do what I want to do." If he feels like spending a month or two in Florida this winter—an attractive notion—he can't.

But he exhibits little apparent regret or frustration about this trade-off. It helps to be, as his son, Jeff, calls him, "the most positive man I've ever met," an admirer of Norman Vincent Peale's *The Power of Positive Thinking*, the mother of all self-help books.

No more inclined to grumble about work than about his health, Jim marches on with acceptance bordering on fatalism. "I'm a firm believer that I'm where I'm supposed to be right now, doing what I'm supposed to do," he says. "And when it's time to do something different, that's what will happen."

Working longer is also in the cards for the people Milton Chavis ushers into his tiny cubicle at the D.C. Office on Aging, though most can't summon the same equanimity as Jim Martin.

Chavis and three other counselors place 600 seniors a year in training programs or jobs, most of them part time. These aren't high-paying positions—McDonald's starts employees at $6.60 to $7 an hour through its McMasters program, and any job offering $9 to $13 an hour constitutes "big-time income," Chavis says—but they make a difference nonetheless.

Clients sometimes tell Chavis that they're doing fine, just feeling a bit restless. "I need to get out of the house," they say. He knows better. Nearly all rely on pensions or Social Security checks that pay less than $1,000 a month. They're mostly women, nearly all African American, some with limited computer skills or physical limitations—the very groups that advocacy groups such as AARP worry most about if government benefits are cut or qualifying ages raised.

So Chavis hooks people up with temp agencies, with universities that need exam proctors, with RFK Stadium and the MCI Center. "I have quite a crew over there working the Mystics and Wizards games"—ticket takers, ushers, food service workers. Two years ago, a national program called Experience Works, which promotes employment for seniors, named him the District's outstanding older worker.

"You won't be able to help everybody," recognizes Chavis, who has one client who is 82. "You just sit here and weep sometimes." But Chavis doesn't really spend much time lamenting. A lifelong District resident (Dunbar High, Class of '55), he's distinguished by unremitting enthusiasm. He's the first one at work each morning, turning on the lights by 7:15, even though the Office on Aging doesn't open for business until 9. He always meets with clients in a suit, tie and highly polished shoes (he's an Air Force veteran). His favorite word is "fantastic!"

This morning, for instance, Howard University is calling, seeking someone to work in the law library. "Oh, fantastic," Chavis burbles, scribbling notes. "Twenty hours? That's fine . . . Beautiful. I really appreciate the call." He has four or five people in mind even before he hangs up the receiver.

He has high hopes, too, for Hosea Myers, who is 66 and, like most clients, has walked in without an appointment. "I did construction work a long time ago, 25 years ago," Myers recounts as the two sit down together. "And I drove a moving van." Now he can't lift much because of a disability; he also needs time to care for his mother. "It's so hard to get on, you know."

Chavis listens quietly. "I could get you something real light," he suggests. "Like cleaning a post office in the morning, 7:30 to 11 or so. I have the forms here . . ."

Eight dollars an hour sounds good to Myers. He'll bring in his résumé—"a little outdated," but Chavis will help him revise it—in a few days. "You're a good man, and I appreciate you," Chavis tells him, clasping Myers's hand. "I'll look for you next week."

Chavis's empathy comes partly from a 29-year career in city government, much of it spent recruiting kids for the federal Job Corps, but also from knowing quite well what it's like to be an older worker who needs a job. "I am just the same," he says. "No different, no better."

He's 68. Ten years ago, as the D.C. Department of Employment Services was facing staff cuts, Chavis—then also president of Local 1000 of the American Federation of Government Employees—walked over to the personnel office. There he learned that between his pension and the Social Security benefits he could collect at 62, his income would soon amount to about $30,000 a year. "I said, Ooh, fine." His wife, Georgia, already retired from an Army administrative job, had a pension, too, worth about $16,000 a year.

The Chavises had no personal savings—they'd grown up in a time and place when work, not investment, was the supposed key to security—but this seemed enough to retire on. At a farewell bash downtown, Milton's friends and co-workers toasted him with champagne, and one colleague sang "I Believe I Can Fly."

"I thought the kids would be gone, and we could have extra," says Georgia. "But it didn't work out that way."

They're sitting at their dining room table at the Fort Chaplin Apartments on East Capitol Street, the complex they downsized into after unloading a four-bedroom house on C Street SE. They'd refinanced their mortgage so often, mostly to pay for parochial schools in Prince George's County for their three children, that the house had become a burden instead of an asset. But this $825-a-month apartment, intended for the two of them after the kids headed off, was affordable.

"I envisioned just she and I hitting the road at our leisure. I'd like to feel I have that kind of freedom."—Milton Chavis, D.C.
Office on Aging

For years, Milton had held a second job as a security guard or janitor in downtown office buildings. Georgia picked him up at 1 or 2 in the morning, then both reported for their day jobs after a few hours' sleep. In retirement, "I envisioned just she and I hitting the road at our leisure," Milton remembers. "I'd like to feel I have that kind of freedom." He also wanted to write about his life, "just for me." Maybe he and Georgia could visit Europe and Africa. Maybe he could complete his own interrupted college studies.

But their parental expenses didn't end, even as two children went to college and then all three enlisted in the Navy. The Chavises found themselves paying off college loans, buying cell phones and sending care packages, reducing the balances on the kids' charge cards to rehab their credit ratings, taking over one son's child support payments for a time. They sent money to their grandchildren. And, Milton says, "we never anticipated that the cost of living would skyrocket the way it has. Food. Gas." In 2000, when a colleague he'd worked with years ago moved to the Office on Aging and offered him a contract, he took it gladly.

Now he's even gladder. To their parents' surprise and puzzlement, the two younger children, 30-year-old Kimberly and 36-year-old Miguel, left the Navy after serving in the Afghanistan and Iraq invasions, and have moved back home. Each is getting a degree at the University of the District of Columbia.

So the Chavises find themselves supporting not two people, but four. Those plastic storage boxes stacked around the living and dining rooms belong to Miguel, who sleeps on the sofa. Kimberly has the second bedroom, shared on weekends with Miguel's daughter Janae, who generally lives with her mother in Maryland.

How long they will remain in residence is a subject of family jokes that aren't entirely jokes. Miguel is completing a bachelor's degree in psychology and vows that, "when he gets everything together, he's going to get a house, and we'll have our own side, our own door," his mother reports. "So, I'm waiting." She and Milton have a good laugh. Kimberly, who expects to finish her master's in counseling next spring and has a full-time security job, feels very conscious of her parents' sacrifices, but she suspects her dad would work anyway, whether she was living at home or not. "With his work ethic, he'll continue to do it," she thinks. "If he felt he was tired, he didn't want to go on, that's another matter."

But Milton does tire at times. He's paid to work from 9 to 3 four days a week, but his early arrival makes for a much longer day, and he sometimes uses his supposed day off to visit prospective employers, lobbying them to hire his clients. When Georgia picks him up after work and drives him home, he takes a three-hour nap so that he can stay up to watch a basketball game or "American Idol." His doctor, concerned about his high blood pressure, keeps upping the dosage of his medication; he has also had a couple of episodes of gout, but he hobbled to work anyway.

He declines to complain about any of this. "That's real negativity," he says. "For me to keep my spirit and my joy, I try not to buy into that." Besides, Milton loves his job, which he calls "my purpose, my mission and my passion, all rolled into one."

He has noticed, however, that "the expectation that one day, you get to sit back and take it easy, sit on the porch and drink iced tea like you see in the movies," is fading. For his clients and, ultimately, perhaps, for himself, "retirement is a myth."

Are Americans willing to peel those "I'm Spending My Children's Inheritance" stickers off their car bumpers and defer retirement?

Some already have, of course.

They might work more for pleasure than profit, like Rita Weiss, who is 70 and still spending 20 hours a week with the 4-year-olds in Washington Hebrew Congregation's preschool program in Potomac. Both she and her husband, Irv, a former library manager now part-timing at Barnes & Noble in Rockville, are drawing federal pensions and could stop working, but why? "We enjoy the people, we enjoy having a purpose. I don't like to shop, and I'd get tired of going to lunch," she says crisply.

Others have less jolly reasons. Stuart Taylor thought it would be "fun" to do a little substitute teaching—two days a week sounded ideal—after he left a 33-year sales career with Procter & Gamble. But in the spring of 2000, he watched P&G's stock price drop by nearly half in a single day: "It cost me literally a million dollars." So, at 65, he's spending three or four days a week in Montgomery County high schools and middle schools.

John Bartlett, a chemical and nuclear engineer about to turn 70, has been an academic, a consultant and an assistant secretary at the Department of Energy. He's one of those people who hoped never to retire; his wife Joan, a psychologist, felt the same way. But five years ago, an auto accident caused her such severe brain damage that she had to relinquish her practice at 58. "It all came apart at about the same time—the market dropped, she had the accident, she lost her career and business," John says. "This is draining the hell out of us."

He connected with the Senior Environmental Employment program, which supplies workers over 55 to environmental agencies, and he now works full time at the EPA's Federal Triangle headquarters. His co-workers are "really capable and intelligent . . . I enjoy the interaction," he says. He also welcomes the modest $12.81-an-hour paycheck. But the great draw is health insurance that covers most of Joan's continuing treatment. "I like to work," John says. "But I am impelled to work."

"We exalt activity and engagement. That's how we maintain vital identities."
—David Ekerdt, gerontologist

The already-mandated increases in the full Social Security age—it's 66 for those now 51 to 62, stepping up to 67 for those born after 1960—may accelerate the uptick in people remaining in the workforce. Many retirement experts expect Congress to raise those ages further, unpopular a move as that would be.

It's also true that certain impediments to continued work already have been eliminated. Mandatory retirement ages are gone—with certain exceptions, like for airline pilots—and there's no longer a prohibitive tax on income earned while receiving Social Security benefits. The traditional "defined-benefit" pensions, which actually provided lower lifetime payments for those who continued to work past retirement age, are fast receding, at least in the private sector. The "defined-contribution" plans replacing them, such as 401(k)s, don't penalize longer careers.

But are those factors enough to make 70 the new 65? The problem is, people like retirement; at least, they say they do.

How retirees actually spend the hours they used to devote to work is a subject researchers are just now tackling. Our society's "busy ethic," a phrase coined by gerontologist David Ekerdt, discourages seniors' lazing about—just as the work ethic does for younger adults. "We exalt activity and engagement," Ekerdt says. "That's how we maintain vital identities." But the Urban Institute's studies show that it doesn't take that much busy-ness to make people happier about retirement.

Beyond 500 hours a year (about 10 hours a week) spent at "productive activities"—defined as family caregiving, formal or informal volunteering, or paid work—there's no additional satisfaction and sometimes a negative effect. A survey that used time diaries to track elderly adults' behavior, collected by researchers at Syracuse University and the University of Calgary, shows quite a few hours eventually shifting from work into personal care and passive pursuits like watching TV.

Still, in a large ongoing national survey called the Health and Retirement Study that began tracking retirees in the mid-'90s, about 60 percent describe themselves as very satisfied, and another big slice as "moderately" satisfied; fewer than 10 percent say they're not satisfied at all. As long as retirement is voluntary and retirees' health holds up, says economist Keith Bender of the University of Wisconsin-Milwaukee, it's a period of contentment. There's much discussion, therefore, of what might persuade us—or force us—to delay it.

Maybe the boomers will stay in their jobs because they need to. Their health care costs keep soaring, and fewer employers offer health insurance for retirees. Their definitions of an acceptably middle-class life are fairly cushy; things their parents considered luxuries, like a second car or a vacation home, are now widely expected as part of "the good life," AARP surveys show. Yet many boomers haven't saved enough. "Maybe a third to a half are on track to maintaining their living standards," says Sara Rix of AARP's Public Policy Institute. "The rest, we should worry about."

Finances, then, may dictate longer work lives. Two years ago, when AARP asked people age 50 to 70 why they were working in retirement, or expected to, the most common responses were predictably upbeat: People wanted to stay mentally and physically active, to "be productive or useful" and "do something fun." When the pollsters forced them to select just one major motivation, however, the most common response became: "need money."

It's possible, too, that there's something peculiar to boomers that will lead them to behave differently from their predecessors, in retirement as in so many things. Perhaps they like their work more than previous generations. In AARP surveys, roughly 80 percent say they plan to work after retirement, most part time. "Their perception of themselves as forever young is tied to having a job," Rix thinks.

Jobs may get a lot easier to come by, too, given the projected labor shortages. The National Older Worker Career Center predicts rising wages for senior workers, along with more flexible conditions. There's also considerable interest in an approach called "phased retirement," in which experienced older workers cut back their hours and ease out of the workplace gradually, while starting to collect some pension benefits.

But skeptics wonder whether the penchant for early retirement can be reversed. Will employers, for example, really prove so welcoming, even if they're faced with shortages?

"We underestimate the amount of age discrimination that's still out there," says Laurie McCann, who litigates such cases for AARP. "The age stereotypes are so ingrained in our psyches. Rather than hire older workers, they'll import workers or offshore jobs." So if boomers do want to stay on the job, "will jobs be there?" And if they want to start a business or tackle an entirely new field, as many say they do, is that a realistic plan? Even the best projections can't answer some of these questions.

> *"The age stereotypes are so ingrained in our psyches."*—Laurie McCann, lawyer for AARP

We do know that retirement is about to become markedly more complicated. The influx of women into the workforce, for instance, will shortly yield the first large-scale female exodus. But at what age? Couples will need to negotiate that: Often younger than their husbands and having spent years at home raising children, wives may not be enthusiastic about retiring at the same time as their spouses.

Finances will also grow more complex. The majority of workers with pensions, instead of merely cashing monthly checks, will have to figure out how to make those big pots of 401(k) money last 20 or 30 years. Yet the data on Americans' financial savvy are not encouraging.

In short, we are heading into unmapped territory.

The grillmeister's steaks already have been passed around when the subject of retirement arises at the Martins' barbecue.

"My thinking has certainly changed," the anesthesiologist at the end of the table declares. "When I was in my late forties, I thought, we'll retire early, we'll have plenty of money, it'll be fine." She even contemplated getting another degree, in art or geology, something new. "Now I'm not sure I can afford to play like that, with the market where it is." She's planning to practice until 65 or beyond.

"I was home with children, so I have to work till I'm 70," says a defense contract administrator. And it's true that an 18-year gap in her work history, plus a divorce, will put a dent in her Social Security income. "I could not afford my condo if I retired."

The conversation soon turns to whether retirement is such a swell idea, anyway. However chirpy people sound in surveys, anthropologists and sociologists point out that this can also be an ambivalent period, that retirees sometimes feel marginalized and isolated, experience loss as well as liberation.

The administrator remembers that when she was laid up after surgery some years back, "I didn't realize how much I'd miss just saying 'Good morning' to the person next to me" at the office.

"A bit of me says, 'Will I lose my mind?'" the anesthesiologist adds. "I can play in my garden, but how am I going to fill my intellectual needs?"

Closer to Jim at the head of the table, two other guests are debating whether Medicare will still be around when they need it.

"They won't take it away," one guy insists.

"But it'll be pared down," says the other. "People start chipping away at it. Things get dicey."

Jim doesn't say much, but as the senior person at the dinner, he certainly has thought about these issues himself, and so has Anna. At 61, her life expectancy is long; she doesn't want to outlive their savings. So she plans to teach another couple of years, but to stop short of 65. "Jim is a good travel companion, and we enjoy being together," she says. "I would like time to travel with him; I hope that's not too late."

The time-versus-money trade-off is no casual matter for those working into their seventies. Because of increased longevity, they're still likely to have years of leisure when they finally leave the workforce, but they're also more apt to encounter illness or disability than they were at 62 or 65. What is the optimal balance, enough money and enough time? When does "too late" begin?

Jim was almost 40 when his mother and father died within months of each other. As he and his sister began cleaning out their parents' Indiana apartment, they found, in a dresser drawer, a collection of small spiral notebooks in which their mother had recorded all the things she wanted to do.

"One had a list of all the movies she wanted to see," Jim remembers. "You could see where she'd marked them off—she put a line through them—and added new ones." She'd only gotten through about a quarter of the titles, however. Other notebooks listed the books she wanted to read and trips she wanted to take, not to terribly exotic destinations, but to Phoenix and the northern Plains, and Turkey Run State Park, which wouldn't even have required leaving Indiana. "But they would put them off, say, 'Okay, we'll go,' and then put them off. And then she died."

"It made an impression on us," Jim says, talking late one evening a few weeks after the barbecue. "It made me not want to put off things."

Portents of mortality hover around him. When he traveled back to Indiana recently for his 53rd high school reunion, 11 of his 58 classmates had died. On the same trip, he visited his 74-year-old sister; she's very ill. For that matter, he's still trying to come to grips with the fact that, while it causes him no discomfort and currently requires no treatment, he does have cancer. "Why did I get leukemia, and what am I supposed to do with it?" he wonders. "There's something I'm supposed to learn from this. I don't know what it is, exactly."

So perhaps he shouldn't defer the things he wants to do.

Yet what kept his working-class parents from visiting Phoenix or seeing more movies, he suspects, was lack of money. In continuing to earn and save, he may be doing the right thing, after all. Right now, he'd rather be able to afford Europe in the spring, he says, than learn Spanish or paint.

In a couple more years, he might feel otherwise. At 73 or 74, he can see himself scaling back to a three-day week. Until then, the watercolors can wait.

Phased Retirement Keeps Employees—and Keeps Them Happy

BY SARAH FISTER GALE
WORKFORCE MANAGEMENT, JULY 1, 2003

When Ron Coulthard turned 60 three years ago, he wanted a change. He had been an English professor for 31 years at Appalachian State University, part of the University of North Carolina system. While he didn't want to continue working full-time, he wasn't quite ready to retire. If he'd been in that quandary just a year before, he wouldn't have had many options, but in late 1998, the university began a phased-retirement pilot program that allows faculty members over the age of 50 to work half-time at half-salary for up to three years while collecting partial pension benefits.

"It was a pretty good deal," says Coulthard, who joined the program and spent the next three years working full-time during the fall term and taking the other eight months off to enjoy his 11-acre mountain property and write an occasional poem. "If they hadn't offered the program, I probably would have stayed a lot longer, for financial reasons alone."

The half-time salary, combined with his pension and a drop to a lower tax bracket, actually increased John Higby's monthly income by several hundred dollars when he joined the same program that year. "It was perfect," says the retired English professor, who opted to work part-time during both terms, which enabled him to teach every day while remaining exempt from committees and university politics. "It was an almost perfect life. I regret that I couldn't do it for a few more years."

The program was a huge success. Today, almost one-third of retiring faculty members at the 16 UNC campuses take advantage of phased retirement, and the concept is slowly catching on in many other public and private organizations.

IRS Presents Obstacles

Low unemployment and rapidly aging baby boomers sparked the push to create programs that allow older workers to ease out of their jobs by reducing the number of hours they work in the years leading up to or just after they reach retirement age. It's an attractive option for individuals because they can continue to earn an income under more flexible terms. And companies benefit from having ongoing access to their most experienced personnel, often at a reduced cost because they work part-time, says Valerie Paginelli, senior retirement consultant at Watson Wyatt, a human resources and risk management consulting firm headquartered in Washington, D.C.

Unfortunately, IRS laws that were designed decades ago to discourage retirees from working make it almost impossible for employees to maintain their previous income level through a combination of social security, pension and paycheck. For example, an earnings test for social security, which was only recently repealed, stated that retirees between 65 and 69 would lose $1 of social security benefits for every $3 they earned above the earnings limit. Even though the Freedom to Work Act of 2000 eliminated the test, pension rules still prohibit companies from giving partial payments to employees who want to reduce their hours before they reach retirement age, says Kyle Brown, retirement counsel for Watson Wyatt. "There are a lot of obstacles to phased retirement, but that's the 600-pound gorilla." (The professors using phased retirement at UNC are in a different situation—they actually have reached retirement age.)

Further, many pension plans state that companies cannot continue to employ individuals and distribute their full pension payments after they reach retirement age, which means that if seniors want their complete benefits, they have to find a job elsewhere.

These laws, combined with the now struggling economy, have made formal phased-retirement programs a rarity in many industries, even though the threat of a skilled-labor shortage increases every year, Paginelli says. At the moment, high unemployment has made this issue a low priority. But she predicts that within five years the rapidly aging workforce and lack of skilled replacements will force organizations to refocus their recruiting efforts on the retention of existing key talent. "When companies forecast the number of people they will have to hire in five years due to retirement and planned growth, it can be staggering. There won't be a large enough volume of workers to replace them."

By 2010, 80 million baby boomers will begin to reach the age of 65. Today, one in three workers is over age 45, and by 2006 the median age of America's workforce will rise to 40.6, up from 30 in the early 1960s. Industries such as nursing and manufacturing are already facing a tremendous loss of expertise as a result of downsizing and a rapidly aging workforce, and other industries will soon follow. However, most companies won't respond until they experience the shock of a mass retirement, Paginelli says. "Pain determines how much energy they invest in reshaping their retirement plans."

> *"There are a lot of obstacles to phased retirement, but that's the 600-pound gorilla."*— Kyle Brown, retirement counsel for Watson Wyatt

Universities Lead Trend

Older organizations are the first to feel the impact of this knowledge loss, which is one reason why public universities were quick to embrace this trend. In 2000, 83 percent of academic institutions reported that 25 percent or more of their faculty were over the age of 50, according to a William M. Mercer study. Of all the industries covered in the study, universities had the oldest employee populations. "If everyone who was eligible retired at once, it would have devastating consequences," says Betsy Brown, associate vice president of academic affairs at UNC, where more than half of the staff is over 55. Phased retirement, which was implemented in 1998, helps Brown spread the loss of veteran staff over several years without disrupting the academic environment.

It's a natural fit for a university because teaching positions can easily be converted to part-time by reducing the class load while still giving students access to experienced professors, she says. It's a relatively cheap and attractive benefit to offer at a time when premiums are increasing and no one is getting raises. "There are no automatic costs to phased retirement, and even those who don't take advantage of it appreciate having the option," she says. And the program benefits the university financially because it frees half of the salaries of the highest-paid faculty to hire new full-time professors, giving the university additional staff for the same personnel costs.

"The program gets rid of old folks like me to make room for the young firebrands who are hot to publish and get much lower salaries," Coulthard says. When he went to part-time, his remaining salary was enough to hire another full-time faculty member. "After 31 years, even in the English department, you build up a big salary from cost-of-living increases alone. Financially, it was beneficial for me and for the university." It also helps the university get out of long-term relationships with less-treasured employees, adds Robert Clark, professor of business management and economics at UNC. Tenured faculty are extremely valuable to the system, but they also have tremendous power over their retirement options. "There is no mandatory retirement age, and if they are tenured it is difficult to encourage them to leave," Clark says. But in order to apply for phased retirement, faculty members must give up tenure and become term employees, setting a course for their departure from the system. "It has dramatically evened out the retirement cycle."

Private companies have been slower to embrace phased retirement because the financial and long-range ramifications are less apparent, Paginelli says. Unless a company has a large number of highly skilled employees who are eligible for retirement, such programs have little obvious impact on the bottom line. "There is savings from a reduction in recruiting and training costs and in retaining the value of experienced employees," she says, "but those benefits are harder to quantify."

Companies that do adopt programs are typically in industries in which knowledge transfer among highly skilled laborers is a challenge. Ultratech, Inc., a maker of photolithography systems in San Jose, California, is one of the few companies in Silicon Valley that offers phased retirement, says Heidi Ordwein, director of human resources. She attributes their initial interest in the program to the company's 25-year history. "Unlike most high-tech companies with youthful workforces, we have employees who have been with us for more than 20 years," she says. "We look at our employees differently than younger companies."

Ultratech implemented phased retirement two years ago to stem a growing loss of retiring employees with critical expertise and knowledge. Employees as young as 50 have the option of reducing their schedule or work periodically on a contract basis. Employees love the program, Ordwein says. And it's a "kick in the pants" for managers who work on what she calls a "truck system approach" to knowledge management: an employee has to "get hit by a truck" before someone else is trained for that job. "Phased retirement forces managers to create a transition plan for retirees and to think about mentoring in a replacement," she says. It also helps retirees remain active in the company and to feel appreciated. "Staying connected is so important. We want our people to know we still value them."

Homemade Retirement Plans

Despite the overwhelming employee support of phased retirement at companies like Ultratech, very few organizations offer it as an option. But that's not stopping retirees from working, Paginelli says. Studies show that many older workers are crafting their own phased-retirement plans, usually by taking full retirement benefits from one employer and going to work for another. With pension rules as they are, it's often in retirees' best interest to work for someone else so that they can maximize their income potential, she says, noting that some companies even take advantage of this situation by targeting retired seniors through their recruiting campaigns. At Republic Parking System in Chattanooga, Tennessee, for example, seniors make up more than 20 percent of the company's 2,000 employees, says Bob Mitchell, senior vice president of human resources at the parking and transportation management company. He prefers hiring seniors because they are more reliable than younger employees, who he says are more likely to call in sick and have a weaker work ethic. "Senior citizens as a group are more dependable. They work because they want to." He has also noticed that they are friendlier and tend to build relationships with regular customers, even though the only contact they have is when customers exit the parking ramp. "They learn about customers' kids and families, and even exchange birthday cards," he says. "They are a great resource, and they represent us well."

Legislators have begun evaluating the efficacy of pension rules, but there's been little drive to push new laws through. Modification is inevitable, but it could be years before significant changes are made, says Anna Rappaport, a consultant for Mercer Human Resource Consulting in Chicago. That means that companies like Republic will continue to have access to a growing pool of highly skilled retirees looking for work. A 1999 AARP survey found that 8 in 10 baby boomers plan to work at least part-time during their retirement. Even though only 16 percent of companies have formal phased-retirement plans, a recent Congressional Research Service paper noted that 20 to 40 percent of workers in their 60s are already working part-time.

"These people want to continue working, even if they have to create their own opportunities," Paginelli says. "If you don't have a phased-retirement plan, they may be taking their talents to the competition."

Doing Homework

BY ROGER FILLION
ROCKY MOUNTAIN NEWS, FEBRUARY 6, 2006

Utah resident Steven Singley used to work in an office across the street from his home. But it took him about 30 minutes to get to his job.

Singley, 41, is a quadriplegic. He gets around in an electric wheelchair. His arms and legs were paralyzed 19 years ago. A pickup he was driving veered off a two-lane road late at night and flipped six times.

To get to his J.C. Penney Co. call center job in suburban Salt Lake City, Singley had to steer his wheelchair out of his condo and across the street. He then would call someone to let him into the building and take him up an elevator so he could get situated at his desk.

Today, it takes Singley, with the help of his girlfriend, about five minutes to set up for his job. He works from a home office in his condo. His employer is Alpine Access Inc., a Golden company whose employees work from home as customer-service agents for other companies.

Singley is a customer-service rep for Office Depot, taking orders for desks, copy paper and chairs. He also helps customers fix orders after an item arrives broken or the wrong product was delivered.

Singley hooked up with Alpine Access last April after the Penney call center closed. He doesn't miss his old commute.

"My disability," he noted, "doesn't allow me to travel easily."

He also likes the flexible work schedule in his new job, particularly when he's had to miss days because of kidney infections linked to his disability.

Singley is among tens of millions of people who work from home, or telecommute. Telecommuting, or telework, has been growing, helped by the broader deployment of high-speed broadband communications and, more recently, the jump in gasoline prices, which has made workers reluctant to drive long distances.

In Singley's case, telework accommodates his disability. In fact, 10 percent of Alpine Access' 7,500 agents are disabled, including a quadriplegic man in Massachusetts who relies on a specially trained capuchin monkey for a helping hand. Almost 5,000 of Alpine Access' home-based agents are in Colorado.

Others telecommute to get time to take care of their young kids—or to spend more time with their family instead of sitting in traffic.

Companies have their own reasons for encouraging the practice. Executives and experts say it saves businesses money on real estate costs and allows a company to continue to operate in the event of a major storm or catastrophe that shutters a central office.

Aids Recruitment and Retention

Executives also say it helps them recruit and retain quality employees—such as educated, married 30-somethings who want a flexible job that allows them to stay home with their kids. The teleworker also might be a military wife or a retiree wanting extra cash.

"The caliber of the people we're getting is better than what you'd get in a regular contact center," said Alpine Access CEO Garth Howard.

Other local companies that promote and rely on telecommuters are Sun Microsystems Inc. in Broomfield and McKesson Health Solutions, a Broomfield health-services unit of McKesson Corp. Elsewhere, JetBlue Airways' 1,400 reservation agents all work from home.

An estimated 45.1 million employed Americans did some type of work at home during the past year, according to research conducted by Dieringer Research Group for ITAC, a telework advisory group linked to the Arizona-based nonprofit WorldatWork.

That was up less than 2 percent from 2004.

But the number of people who are full-time employees and allowed to work from home at least one day a month increased by 30 percent, to 9.9 million.

Dieringer says the jump could be the result of a strengthening economy and "an increasing acceptance by post-recession employers to permit telework."

For McKesson Health Solutions, a home-based work force allowed it to cut costs and land quality applicants.

McKesson serves commercial and government health care customers, including state Medicaid programs.

It relies on nurses who field incoming calls from patients about acute medical conditions such as possible heart attacks or injuries. The nurses also make outbound calls to Medicaid or commercial health-plan patients to educate them about specific chronic illnesses they might have. A diabetic, for example, might learn proper blood-sugar levels.

McKesson started moving toward a home-based work force about 1 1/2 years ago. The company was operating call centers. But they were pricey to build and operate.

The company reckoned it would cost $300,000 to $500,000 up front to build a new medium-sized center for about 50 agents. It would then cost $100,000 a year to run.

McKesson also was finding it tough to recruit nurses for its call centers. They were in short supply. And hospitals were dangling bonuses to lure nurses aboard.

"We were dealing with a nursing shortage where everybody was offering something to attract that nurse," said Mike Modiz, a McKesson vice president.

So company officials pondered what could they offer.

Bingo!

"The ability to work from home was something I could offer and a hospital could not," Modiz said.

The strategy worked. About a year ago, McKesson put an ad in a Sacramento paper for nursing jobs at a call center there.

"We had one contact from that ad," Modiz said.

But when McKesson again ran the ad and encouraged nurses to ask about McKesson's work-from-home program, the company got nearly 400 responses.

"We were dealing with a nursing shortage where everybody was offering something to attract that nurse."—Mike Modiz, vice president, **McKesson Health Solutions**

"We got flooded," Modiz said.

Today, McKesson has 400 home-based nurses nationwide. It still operates five call centers, including one in Broomfield (that's down from a peak of seven).

According to McKesson, annual attrition among its home-based nurses is 10 percent—vs. 30 percent among call-center nurses.

To be sure, the number of telecommuters hasn't followed a straight upward trajectory—particularly after the Internet bubble burst in 2000.

According to research firm IDC, which calculates telework using a different formula than Dieringer Research, the estimated number of telecommuting households totaled some 9 million in 2000.

That figure covers the number of households where someone worked at least three days a month from home.

By 2002, the number edged up to 9.1 million. It then fell to 8.7 million in 2003 before rising again to 9.1 million by 2005.

Explaining the drop-off, IDC analyst Merle Sandler said: "With the downturn in the economy, a lot of people wanted to be seen at the office."

At Sun Microsystems in Broomfield, however, it isn't necessary to be seen. The company employs about 4,700 in the area, following its purchase of Louisville-based Storage Technology Corp. Employees have the option to work from home, either part time or most of the time.

"The opportunity is available to just about anybody in the company to consider it," said David Raduziner, Sun's senior director of workplace resources. "We have been very active in providing flexibility for our work force for over 10 years."

Among the company's local work force, more than 530 work from home at least two to three days a week. When they need to work at Sun's campus, these people reserve a work space through an online reservation system.

"You can choose the building. You can choose the floor. You can choose a cubicle or an enclosed office," said Raduziner, who works mainly from a home office above his Boulder garage.

Companywide, Sun estimates its work-at-home program saved it $69 million last year in the way of real estate and information technology costs.

"It's Not for Everybody"

Telecommuting, however, doesn't work in all situations, according to experts. Take the employee.

"Can they really be trusted to get the job done with less supervision?" asked Chuck Wilsker, CEO of the Telework Coalition, a nonprofit that advocates telework.

Wilsker said poor candidates are people who are "time-oriented"— they look at their watches to see how soon it is until quitting time. Better candidates are those who are "task oriented" and want to get the job done.

"It's not for everybody," Wilsker said.

Also, prospective teleworkers shouldn't expect the company to foot the bill for a brand-new home office with all the high-tech trimmings.

In the case of Alpine Access, for example, the company says on its Web site that agents are required to have:

- A "reliable" personal computer with at least a Windows 98 Second Edition operating system.
- A subscription to a "reliable high-speed" Internet service.
- The ability to be on the Internet and the phone at the same time, without the use of a cell phone or an Internet-based phone.
- A corded headset with a noise-canceling microphone.

But those requirements weren't a deal killer for the wheelchair-bound Singley. The company's flexible work arrangement could allow him to some day finish his studies in computer-aided drafting and design. Earlier, he was forced to put those studies on hold.

"It gave me an opportunity to look at going to school and finishing my degree," Singley said.

Firms Go High-Tech to Screen Applicants

By Karen Dybis
The Detroit News, June 22, 2004

Employers are becoming bloodhounds when it comes to digging up resume fudging, criminal records, even the overdue bills of potential hires.

In today's risk-conscious workplace, job seekers face increasingly invasive inspections, including personality tests designed to identify whether someone is likely to blow off work or dip into the till.

Is Big Brother working overtime? It depends on whom you ask. Companies say more sophisticated screening methods are crucial to avoiding bad hires who can cripple productivity or even lead to lawsuits.

Some job seekers, though, wonder what ever happened to second chances and fresh starts.

Linda Durham, a 50-year-old Detroiter, said she lost a salaried auditing job when a background check showed she had a poor credit history and credit card debt.

"That did hurt. If I had gotten the earnings I needed, I could have gotten straightened out," said Durham, who now works as a mortgage loan officer on commission. "There's nothing you can do. Everyone is doing it now."

During the last decade, employment screening has evolved into a billion-dollar business. Technology has made the process easier, faster and relatively inexpensive. For as little as $25 and a few hours, screening companies with access to millions of personal public records can find out nearly anything about a potential hire.

"These days, we take hiring very seriously," said Kerry Christopher, a spokesman for General Motors Corp., which puts salaried employees through a three-step interview process—including problem-solving role playing—before extending an offer. Drug tests and background checks follow.

At grocer Spartan Stores, its 54 retail outlets use a high-tech application process to ask probing psychological questions, such as whether candidates believe it is OK to give friends a discount. Answer the wrong way, and the Grand Rapids chain could label you as "red" or a poor potential hire.

Fear of hiring the wrong person convinces many businesses to retain ChoicePoint Inc., Kroll Inc. of New York, First Advantage Corp. of St. Petersburg, Fla., or Automatic Data Processing's Screening and Selection Services, some of the nation's largest screening companies.

"How do you know that the person sitting in the next cubicle is really who they say they are?" said Chuck Jones, spokesman for ChoicePoint Inc., which boasts a data warehouse of more than 17 billion public records.

Last year, ChoicePoint of Alpharetta, Ga. conducted 6 million background checks. ADP of Roseland, N.J., performed more than 3.7 million checks last year, up 26 percent from 2002.

"Business is booming," said Christian Felton, a private investigator and vice president of business development for A.S.K. Services Inc. in Canton Township, a records research company.

Felton said screening requests have increased during the past three to four months as Michigan's economy improved. He said most companies are interested in background checks for criminal, driving and educational histories.

Counter Checks

Workers can even check themselves out. For $24.95, ChoicePoint will run a background check on your resume, showing potential employers it has been prescreened to confirm its accuracy. If a bad review is holding you back, Rochester Hills–based Allison & Taylor Inc. will call your references to see what they say about you at a cost of about $75.

Industry officials justify the intrusive screening by pointing to a minefield of problems that can stem from a mis-hire. Forgoing background checks has put some companies on the losing end of negligent-hiring lawsuits with courts noting that employers should have discovered issues such as a violent past.

High-profile slips also have made employee screens a priority for large, public companies. For example, handgun maker Smith & Wesson Holding Corp. chairman, James J. Minder Jr., resigned earlier this year when his conviction for a series of Metro Detroit armed robberies was discovered.

"Every business at every level has a responsibility to know as much as they possibly can about the people they're hiring or sending into your home," said William Greenblatt, CEO of New York–based Sterling Testing Systems Inc., another nationwide screening service.

ChoicePoint, Sterling and others tell many of these stories and quote startling employment statistics: One in 10 people have a criminal history. Between 30 percent to 40 percent of all resumes contain mistakes, like the wrong job title or the months of employment.

ADP says it found that half of all applicants showed inconsistencies on their resumes or a judgment, lien or bankruptcy in their backgrounds.

These numbers point to why background screening has grown at nearly 10 percent annually during the last decade, according to Lehman Brothers analyst Jeffrey T. Kessler.

Heavy Screening

In southeastern Michigan, half of the 270 companies surveyed by the American Society of Employers said they conduct criminal record checks. Some 82 percent check a potential employee's references, said Kevin Marrs, director of survey services.

However, Kessler and others estimate only 20 to 25 percent of all companies do a full background check on job candidates, looking beyond references and into indentity verification, driving records, criminal histories or credit reports.

Privacy advocates worry companies who do background checks have too much access to an individual's private information. However, industry experts say there are safeguards in place. For example, employers must get a candidate's permission to use certain consumer reports through the Fair Credit Reporting Act.

Industries that handle consumer finances such as banking or insurance have long done background checks on their employees as have most government agencies. Today, companies that invest heavily in training or have high turnover rates are looking at background screening as a cost-cutting measure.

Spartan Stores, for example, receives about 25,000 job applications annually at its 54 stores, said Beth Baumgartner, regional human resource manager for the grocery store chain. Since it started using the computerized job application process in 2002—which includes psychological screening—Spartan has lowered its turnover rate from nearly 100 percent to about 59 percent.

Privacy advocates worry companies who do background checks have too much access to an individual's private information.

The kiosks are created by Unicru Inc., a Beaverton, Ore.–based company that specializes in employee screening software, online applications and systems like the employment kiosks that are also used by CVS Corp., Kroger Co. and Blockbuster Inc.

The Unicru system had unexpected benefits, Baumgartner said. Paper applications are sometimes hard to get at a busy store, but the kiosks are open to every candidate. As a result, the company feels it has reduced the risk of a lawsuit by the Equal Employment Opportunity Commission for discrimination, Baumgartner said.

Holiday Market in Royal Oak still relies on old-fashioned interviews. People who made mistakes can be good employees given the chance, said Tom Violante Jr., store director for the family-owned grocer.

"Background checks take management out of the equation. We watch an employee's performance and consider their values to see if they're a good fit," he said. "They either stay and advance or move on."

Yes, the Boss Is . . . Watching

By Patricia Kitchen
Newsday, February 19, 2006

An employee enters an unauthorized area of the company, his smart-chip badge triggering a hidden surveillance camera. That sends an alert to a security officer, who uses his laptop or cell phone to monitor what the intruder is up to.

Once the realm of Tom Cruise movies, scenes such as this one are playing out now at a worksite near you.

What's more, employer surveillance of workers and property extends beyond the video screen: The boss can tell just what Web sites you've visited on office computers, the content of e-mail you haven't even sent, even your every move through cell phones equipped with global positioning. And coming soon: Employee identification through biometrics—measuring such biological components as fingerprints and voice pattern—as well as grain-of-wheat–sized chips implanted under the skin, turning you, in effect, into an EZPass.

All of which might lead the unsuspecting employee to ask: Just what privacy rights do I have when it comes to electronic monitoring? Darn few, says L. Camille Hebert, law professor at Ohio State University and author of "Employee Privacy Law" (Thomson West).

Certainly, bosses can cite significant reasons for tracking worker activity: Monitoring can go a long way toward cutting down on sexual harassment, workplace accidents and goofing off. Plus, in lawsuits, courts expect employers to be able to hand over electronic evidence. So such surveillance is on the increase: The use of video monitoring for theft, violence and sabotage rose last year to 51 percent of 526 employers surveyed by the American Management Association and ePolicy Institute; only 33 percent were using such monitoring four years earlier. And research company Frost & Sullivan estimates that by 2010, the surveillance and video technology industry will be an $8.64 billion business—more than double what it was in 2003.

The federal Electronic Communications Privacy Act of 1986—amended in 2001—gives employers what privacy experts call pretty much carte blanche. Nancy Flynn, executive director of the ePolicy Institute in Columbus, Ohio, says the provisions of the act can be translated this way: "The computer system is the property of the employer and as such the employer has the right to monitor Internet activity and e-mail. Employees should have no reasonable expectation to privacy."

The Cost in Morale

Still, the exchange of privacy for more efficiency and security carries costs when it comes to employee morale, says Lewis Maltby, president of the National Workrights Institute in Princeton, N.J. He poses these real and potential situations: A woman who found out she was pregnant, visited an expectant-mothers' Web site and then got confronted by her boss later that day. Or a worker who sends her doctor an e-mail containing terminology that could also have sexual meaning. Or those subjected to video surveillance in restrooms or changing rooms.

Most employers who use forms of surveillance say they notify their employees. The American Management/ePolicy Institute research found that 80 percent let workers know they're being monitored for computer content, keystrokes and keyboard time; 82 percent let them know computer files are stored and reviewed; 86 percent, that e-mail is tracked; and 89 percent, that Web visits are monitored.

Most members of the human resources committee of the Hauppauge Industrial Association have monitoring policies, said Patty O'Connell, committee co-chairwoman and human resources vice president of People's Alliance Federal Credit Union, headquartered in Hauppauge. That institution's policy is clearly stated, she said, and covers all types of information systems, including faxing. And, as a financial institution, it does engage in video monitoring.

> *"A thin line exists between surveillance and voyeurism."*
> —Jeremy Gruber, legal director, National Workrights Institute

When used irresponsibly, that's the most invasive form of electronic surveillance, said Jeremy Gruber, legal director of the National Workrights Institute based in Princeton, N.J.

Before and after work, when her office at Salem State College in Massachusetts was empty, secretary Gail Nelson would change in and out of exercise clothes behind a tall partition. Her boss never told her she was being captured on tape by a hidden camera that had been set up to monitor for intruders.

She filed a lawsuit and lost the case. In a brief in support of her appeal, Gruber wrote: "Some cameras are entirely appropriate. Security cameras in stairwells and parking garages make us all safer without intruding on privacy. But employers often install cameras in areas that are indefensible . . . where employees undress, including bathrooms, locker rooms, sometimes inside the stalls themselves. . . . A thin line exists between surveillance and voyeurism."

Just three states—California, New York and Rhode Island—have statutes prohibiting video monitoring of workplace restrooms or other areas where employees undress.

Ed Wolm, 33, said that last year the staff in his network maintenance department at Cablevision were given cell phones that he said were equipped with GPS tracking. He said the system could not be de-activated as long as the phone was on—and it had to be on when workers were on call on their off time—so the belief was the company could monitor their whereabouts round the clock.

His feeling was "the company didn't trust you." At the time, he was engaged in union organizing activity for Local 1049, International Brotherhood of Electrical Workers, and he said the potential for monitoring of location as well as numbers dialed had a chilling effect. He has since resigned and is now an apprentice lineman with Local 1049.

Though some cell phone devices come with GPS capability, additional software is necessary before an employer can track employee whereabouts and the company does not have that, said a Cablevision spokesperson, who added: "We don't monitor employee whereabouts."

Although some observers maintain the employee has drawn the short end of the stick in this age of surveillance, Craig Cornish, an attorney in Colorado Springs, Colo., with expertise in workplace privacy, says that's yet to be seen. Yes, he says, some courts "bend over backward to support the employer, but that's not universally true." And he said that so far, no case has reached the ultimate arbiter, the U.S. Supreme Court. Lewis Maltby of the National Workrights Institute points to The Employee Changing Room Privacy Act (HR582) that's been introduced in the U.S. House of Representatives, with the goal of prohibiting restroom and changing room video surveillance.

Serving a Purpose

Despite its potential for abuse, electronic monitoring can and does serve valuable workplace purposes. "Like everything—there's a good side and a bad," says Richard Soloway, chairman of NAPCO Security Inc. in Amityville, which manufactures site access and surveillance equipment.

He said he convenes think tanks for quarterly discussions for trends in corporate security and problem-solving amid privacy concerns.

Where It Might Work

Supporters of workplace surveillance point to evidence of its value:

Fourteen nursing home employees in Rochester were charged last month by State Attorney General Eliot Spitzer with fraud and falsifying records because they had moved call bells out of patients' reach so they could watch television or socialize. Their activity was captured when the room of a 70-year-old man with dementia was monitored through video surveillance cameras.

Such cameras can spot the license plate of a reported domestic violence abuser if he drives into the company parking lot, Soloway said; and a security officer at one Texas manufacturer noticed and reported boxes piled high on inventory shelves that were about to topple over, thus averting possible injury to workers.

Such systems are a deterrent to goofing off online, said Doug Fowler, president of SpectorSoft, a Vero Beach, Fla.–based Internet monitoring software maker. His Web site features a case study from a client, First National Bank of Long Island, which quotes the bank's information technology services manager as saying of employees, "A cup of coffee and checking the news online for five minutes in the morning, that's not a big thing. . . . But the bridal registry or tiffany.com for two and a half hours a day . . . take it easy!"

And security measures on the horizon have Maltby concerned. Two security professionals in Cincinnati voluntarily had tiny radio frequency identification chips embedded in their arms—to forgo carrying worker identification cards. Using such chips for recognition only is harmless enough, says Maltby. But long-term? "It's bad enough some employees have to carry a GPS tracking device in their hands. The thought of having the device implanted in your body is frightening."

Another concern—blogs, said O'Connell, a subject discussed at the most recent HIA committee meeting. Flynn agreed that employers need to learn more about blog monitoring applications, as well as become familiar with blog search engines—such as Technorati.com, Daypop.com and Blogpulse.com—where they can plug in the company name, names of executives and products to see just what's being said about them.

"Blogs," she says, "open up the business to all of the same risks posed by e-mails and instant messaging and Internet use."

Appendix

Tomorrow's Jobs

From Occupational Outlook Handbook, 2006–07 Edition
U.S. Department of Labor, Bureau of Labor Statistics, Bulletin 2600

Occupation

Expansion of service-providing industries is expected to continue, creating demand for many occupations. However, projected job growth varies among major occupational groups (Chart 6).

Professional and Related Occupations

Professional and related occupations will grow the fastest and add more new jobs than any other major occupational group. Over the 2004-14 period, a 21.2-percent increase in the number of professional and related jobs is projected, which translates into 6 million new jobs. Professional and related workers perform a wide variety of duties, and are employed throughout private industry and government. About three-quarters of the job growth will come from three groups of professional occupations—computer and mathematical occupations, healthcare practitioners and technical occupations, and education, training, and library occupations—which will add 4.5 million jobs combined.

Service Occupations

Service workers perform services for the public. Employment in service occupations is projected to increase by 5.3 million, or 19 percent, the second largest numerical gain and second highest rate of growth among the major occupational groups. Food preparation and serving related occupations are expected to add the most jobs among the service occupations, 1.7 million by 2014. However, healthcare support occupations are expected to grow the fastest, 33.3 percent, adding 1.2 million new jobs.

Management, Business, and Financial Occupations

Workers in management, business, and financial occupations plan and direct the activities of business, government, and other organizations. Their employment is expected to increase by 2.2 million, or 14.4 percent, by 2014. Among managers, the numbers of preschool and childcare center/program educational administrators and of computer and information systems managers will grow the fastest, by 27.9 percent and 25.9 percent, respectively. General and operations managers will add the most new jobs, 308,000, by 2014. Farmers and ranchers are the only workers in this major occupational group

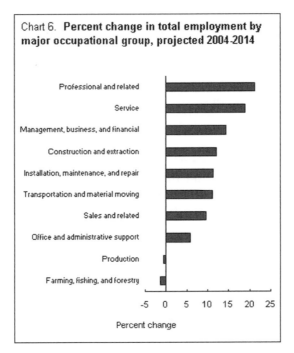

Chart 6. **Percent change in total employment by major occupational group, projected 2004-2014**

whose numbers are expected to decline, losing 155,000 jobs. Among business and financial occupations, accountants and auditors and management analysts will add the most jobs, 386,000 combined. Employment, recruitment, and placement specialists and personal financial advisors will be the fastest growing occupations in this group, with job increases of 30.5 percent and 25.9 percent, respectively.

Construction and Extraction Occupations

Construction and extraction workers construct new residential and commercial buildings, and also work in mines, quarries, and oil and gas fields. Employment of these workers is expected to grow 12 percent, adding 931,000 new jobs. Construction trades and related workers will account for more than three-fourths of these new jobs, 699,000, by 2014. Many extraction occupations will decline, reflecting overall employment losses in the mining and oil and gas extraction industries.

Installation, Maintenance, and Repair Occupations

Workers in installation, maintenance, and repair occupations install new equipment and maintain and repair older equipment. These occupations will add 657,000 jobs by 2014, growing by 11.4 percent. Automotive service technicians and mechanics and general maintenance and repair workers will account for half of all new installation, maintenance, and repair jobs. The fastest growth rate will be among security and fire alarm systems installers, an occupation that is expected to grow 21.7 percent over the 2004–14 period.

Transportation and Material Moving Occupations

Transportation and material moving workers transport people and materials by land, sea, or air. The number of these workers should grow 11.1 percent, accounting for 1.1 million additional jobs by 2014. Among transportation occupations, motor vehicle operators will add the most jobs, 629,000. Material moving occupations will grow 8.3 percent and will add 405,000 jobs. Rail transportation occupations are the only group in which employment is projected to decline, by 1.1 percent, through 2014.

Sales and Related Occupations

Sales and related workers transfer goods and services among businesses and consumers. Sales and related occupations are expected to add 1.5 million new jobs by 2014, growing by 9.6 percent. The majority of these jobs will be among retail salespersons and cashiers, occupations that will add 849,000 jobs combined.

Office and Administrative Support Occupations.

Office and administrative support workers perform the day-to-day activities of the office, such as preparing and filing documents, dealing with the public, and distributing information. Employment in these occupations is expected to grow by 5.8 percent, adding 1.4 million new jobs by 2014. Customer service representatives will add the most new jobs, 471,000. Desktop publishers will be among the fastest growing occupations in this group, increasing by 23.2 percent over the decade. However, due to rising productivity and increased automation, office and administrative support occupations also account for 11 of the 20 occupations with the largest employment declines.

Farming, Fishing, and Forestry Occupations

Farming, fishing, and forestry workers cultivate plants, breed and raise livestock, and catch animals. These occupations will decline 1.3 percent and lose 13,000 jobs by 2014. Agricultural workers, including farmworkers and laborers, accounted for the overwhelming majority of new jobs in this group. The number of fishing and hunting workers is expected to decline, by 16.6, percent, while the number of logging workers is expected to increase by less than 1 percent.

Production Occupations

Production workers are employed mainly in manufacturing, where they assemble goods and operate plants. Production occupations are expected to decline less than 1 percent, losing 79,000 jobs by 2014. Jobs will be created for many production occupations, including food processing workers, machinists, and welders, cutters, solderers, and brazers. Textile, apparel, and furnishings occupations, as well as assemblers and fabricators, will account for much of the job losses among production occupations.

Among all occupations in the economy, computer and healthcare occupations are expected to grow the fastest over the projection period (Chart 7). In fact, healthcare occupations make up 12 of the 20 fastest growing occupations, while computer occupations account for 5 out of the 20 fastest growing occupations in the economy. In addition to high growth rates, these 17 computer and healthcare occupations combined will add more than 1.8 million new jobs. High growth rates among computer and healthcare occupations reflect projected rapid growth in the computer and data processing and health services industries.

The 20 occupations listed in Chart 8, 7.1 million combined, over the 2004–14 period. The occupations with the largest numerical increases cover a wider range of occupational categories than do those occupations with the fastest growth rates. Health occupations will account for some of these increases in employment, as well as occupations in education, sales, transportation, office and administrative support, and food service. Many of these occupations are very large, and will create more new jobs than will those with high growth rates. Only 3 out of the 20 fastest growing occupations—home health aides, personal and home care aides, and computer software application engineers—also are projected to be among the 20 occupations with the largest numerical increases in employment.

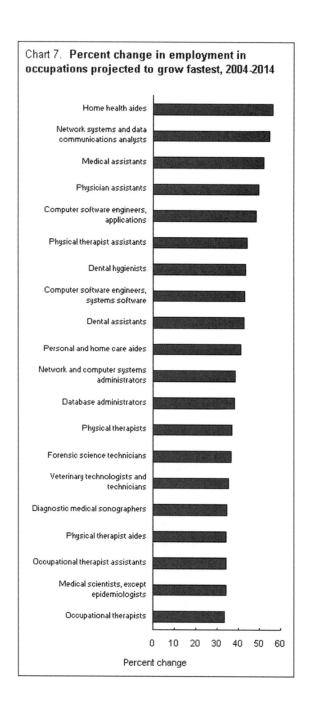

Chart 7. **Percent change in employment in occupations projected to grow fastest, 2004-2014**

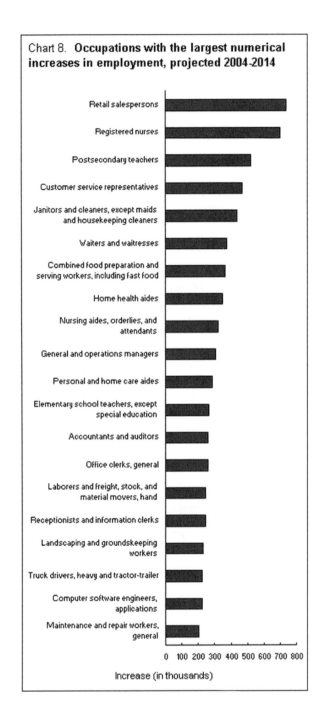

Bibliography

Books

Appelbaum, Eileen, Annette Bernhardt, and Richard J. Murnane, eds. *Low-Wage America: How Employers Are Reshaping Opportunity in the Workplace.* New York: Russell Sage, 2003.

Avery, Christine, and Diane Zabel. *The Flexible Workplace: A Sourcebook of Information and Research.* Westport, Conn.: Quorum, 2001.

Blau, Francine D., Marianne A. Ferber, and Anne E. Winkler. *The Economics of Women, Men, and Work.* 5th ed. Upper Saddle River, N.J.: Prentice, 2005.

Ciulla, Joanne B. *The Working Life: The Promise and Betrayal of Modern Work.* New York: Three Rivers, 2001.

Cooper, Cary L., and Ronald J. Burke, eds. *The New World of Work: Challenges and Opportunities.* Malden, Mass.: Blackwell, 2002.

Dobbs, Lou. *Exporting America: Why Corporate Greed Is Shipping American Jobs Overseas.* New York: Warner, 2004.

Dyer, Susan K., ed. *Women at Work.* Washington, D.C.: American Association of University Women, 2003.

Ehrenreich, Barbara. *Bait and Switch: The (Futile) Pursuit of the American Dream.* New York: Metropolitan, 2005.

Ehrenreich, Barbara. *Nickel and Dimed: On (Not) Getting By in America.* New York: Metropolitan, 2002.

Fraser, Jill Andresky. *White-Collar Sweatshop: The Deterioration of Work and Its Rewards in Corporate America.* New York: Norton, 2001.

Freeman, Richard, and Peter Gottschalk, eds. *Generating Jobs: How to Increase Demand for Less-Skilled Workers.* New York: Russell Sage, 1998.

Friedman, Thomas L. *The World Is Flat: A Brief History of the Twenty-First Century.* New York: Farrar, 2005.

Gray, Kenneth C., and Edwin L. Herr. *Other Ways to Win: Creating Alternatives for High School Graduates.* 2nd ed. Thousand Oaks, Calif.: Corwin, 2000.

Hayworth, J. D, with Joseph J. Eule. *Whatever It Takes: Illegal Immigration, Border Security, and the War on Terror.* Washington, D.C.: Regnery, 2006.

Immergluck, Daniel. *Neighborhood Jobs, Race, and Skills: Urban Unemployment and Commuting.* New York: Garland, 1998.

Klein, Michael W., Scott Schuh, and Robert K. Triest, eds. *Job Creation, Job Destruction, and International Competition.* Kalamazoo, Mich.: W. E. Upjohn, 2003.

Krueger, Alan B., and Robert M. Solow, eds. *The Roaring Nineties: Can Full Employment Be Sustained?* New York: Russell Sage, 2001.

Lane, Frederick S. *The Naked Employee: How Technology Is Compromising Workplace Privacy.* New York: AMACOM, 2003.

LeRoy, Greg. *The Great American Jobs Scam: Corporate Tax Dodging and the Myth of Job Creation*. San Francisco: Berrett-Koehler, 2005.

Lydersen, Kari. *Out of the Sea and into the Fire: Immigration from Latin America to the U.S. in the Global Age*. Monroe, Me.: Common Courage, 2005.

Pollin, Robert, and Stephanie Luce. *The Living Wage: Building a Fair Economy*. New York: New Press, 1998.

Poundstone, William. *How Would You Move Mount Fuji?: Microsoft's Cult of the Puzzle: How the World's Smartest Companies Select the Most Creative Thinkers*. Boston: Little, Brown, 2003.

Reich, Robert B. *The Future of Success: Working and Living in the New Economy*. New York: Knopf, 2001.

Rosenbaum, James E. *Beyond College for All: Career Paths for the Forgotten Half*. New York: Russell Sage, 2001.

Ross, Andrew. *No-Collar: The Humane Workplace and Its Hidden Costs*. New York: Basic, 2003.

Smith, Vicki. *Crossing the Great Divide: Worker Risk and Opportunity in the New Economy*. Ithaca, N.Y.: ILR, 2001.

Uchitelle, Louis. *The Disposable American: Layoffs and Their Consequences*. New York: Knopf, 2006.

Williams, Joan. *Unbending Gender: Why Family and Work Conflict and What to Do about It*. New York: Oxford, 2000.

Web Sites

Readers seeking additional information about employment issues in the United States may wish to refer to the following Web sites, all of which were operational as of this writing.

American Enterprise Institute

www.aei.org

Though broad in scope, the site of the American Enterprise Institute houses hundreds of publications related to jobs and other economic issues and treats these and other subjects from a conservative position. The site draws on a wide range of statistical material and is frequently updated to address topics of current interest.

Brookings Institution

www.brookings.org

A long-established and broadly influential research and policy organization offering detailed analyses of current issues, including virtually every topic covered in this book.

Bureau of Labor Statistics

www.bls.gov

The Bureau of Labor Statistics, a division of the U.S. Department of Labor, is perhaps the most commonly cited source for current and historical data related to jobs in the United States. The site offers stand-alone data—such as an up-to-date chart of the latest information available on a number of key economic indicators—as well as electronic versions of Bureau publications.

Cato Institute

www.cato.org

The Cato Institute provides research and policy-related information on a variety of economic topics. Some particular areas of expertise related to jobs include papers on immigration, taxation, and free trade and its effect on employment.

Economic Policy Institute

www.epi.org

A source for left-leaning economic information, with a particular interest in jobs and job-related issues, the Economic Policy Institute's site provides access to a wealth of Institute publications, ranging from brief policy papers to detailed analyses, and draws on current statistics from both original research and well-respected sources such as the Bureau of Labor Statistics. The Institute also sponsors a site focused exclusively on jobs, *www.jobwatch.org*.

Good Jobs First

www.goodjobsfirst.org

Good Jobs First opposes many of the tax abatements used around the country to attract businesses and create jobs, and this site includes policy information, research, and analytical writing supporting that mission.

Living Wage Resource Center

www.livingwagecampaign.org

A product of the Association of Community Organizations for Reform Now (ACORN), the Living Wage Resource Center is a source for information supporting living wage campaigns. The site offers a history of the movement and provides activists with a number of resources. A related site, *www.raisewages.org*, gives up-to-date information on particular living wage campaigns across the country.

TechsUnite

www.techsunite.org

Sponsored by the Communication Workers of America union and other groups, TechsUnite is a source for information critical of outsourcing, particularly in the information technology sector. Perhaps the site's most useful feature is its "Offshore Tracker," which gives figures estimating the number of American jobs lost to firms in other countries.

Urban Institute

www.urban.org

Less partisan than similar research and policy organizations, the Urban Institute offers detailed information on a number of issues related to jobs, including some areas not covered elsewhere, such as disabilities and job training.

Additional Periodical Articles with Abstracts

More information about American employment and related subjects can be found in the following articles. Readers who require a more comprehensive selection are advised to consult the *Readers' Guide Abstracts*, *Social Sciences Index*, and other H. W. Wilson publications.

Jobfull Recovery. Brian S. Wesbury. *The American Spectator*, v. 37 pp34–35 May 2004.

According to Wesbury, the so-called jobless recovery that had obtained for the last few years ended by May 2004. Payroll employment data, indicating that employment in March increased by 308,000, the most powerful gain in four years, are now giving the same message as other economic data—that the U.S. economy is becoming increasingly vigorous. Wesbury argues that President Bush's 2003 tax cut is driving this growth because it inspired the country's entrepreneurial spirit by reducing taxes on income, capital gains, and dividends. For Bush, who has been politically attacked for job losses, this has been very positive news. Wesbury also suggests that Gregory Mankiw, chairman of the President's Council of Economic Advisers, may have been right when he predicted that there would be 2.6 million new jobs created this year.

Brain Circulation: How High-Skill Immigration Makes Everyone Better Off. AnnaLee Saxenian. *Brookings Review*, pp28–31 Winter 2002.

Saxenian states that the United States and other countries gain from what she terms the brain circulation involved in high-skilled immigration. While immigration is a sharply divisive issue in the U.S., the focus is almost exclusively on less-skilled immigrants. Saxenian argues that entrepreneurial activities of immigrants in Silicon Valley signal that immigration and free trade have clear benefits. Saxenian concludes that the U.S. should allow more skilled workers to immigrate and, at the same, better educate the people already in the country.

What's in a Name for Black Job Seekers? Robert J. Barro. *Business Week*, p24 November 3, 2003.

Barro discusses the findings of economists Roland G. Fryer Jr. and Steven D. Levitt, who have noted that children's names are another area in which there is a large divide between blacks and whites in America. Their research, in the form of a working paper from the National Bureau of Economic Research, was inspired by so-called audit studies, started in Britain in 1970, revealing that potential employers systematically discriminated against job seekers with résumés that had minority-sounding names. Fryer and Levitt conclude, however, that in America, the black-white differences in naming are due to disparities in socioeconomic conditions of blacks and whites rather than an independent cause of disparities. It is true that employers may be racially discriminating, but once Fryer and Levitt factor in parents' socioeconomic status, they find that a person's name no longer predicts much about later economic scenarios.

The Easiest Commute of All. Michelle Conlin. *Business Week*, pp78–80 December 12, 2005.

The numbers of remote workers are growing, Conlin notes, as companies see the logic in releasing them from their obligation to work on site. Currently, about 12 percent of the U.S. workforce qualifies as "distributed" workers, according to Charles Grantham and James Ware, executive producers of Work Design Collaborative, although in urban areas they estimate that figure is closer to 15 percent. Distributed workers are those who have no permanent office at their companies, preferring to work from spaces such as cafés, airport lounges, high school stadium bleachers, or client conference rooms. At IBM, for example, 40 percent of the staff has no office at the company, while at AT&T, one-third of managers work off site. The growth of globalization, independent contractors, long commutes, pricey gas, and the broadband-connected micropolis are all continuing to enlarge the ranks of the location-neutral, particularly at troubled tech companies for which the cost savings can be a godsend.

Beyond the Mall. Jennifer Nelson. *Career World*, v. 34 pp18–21 October 2005.

Nationwide, around 40 percent of teenagers ages 16 to 19 have a part-time job. Retail positions and jobs at burger joints are the jobs teens have traditionally gravitated toward, but those who want to consider future career options or work with something they have a passion for should look further afield. Jennifer Nelson gathers stories from teens and suggestions from experts in order to suggest how these early employment experiences might be used to the best possible advantage.

Easing the Exit. David W. Leslie and Natasha Janson. *Change*, v. 37 pp40–47 November/December 2005.

The writers discuss a 2003–2004 study they conducted on the experience of academics at institutions with phased retirement. Phased retirement policies, they observe, vary significantly in their appeal to potential retirees and have rarely been used by faculty except where they have been offered remarkably generous financial packages. They contend, however, that when phased retirement schemes are used, they help individuals to overcome their concerns about giving up the social, psychological, and professional supports that come with a successful career. They also note that institutions offering "phased retirement" expressed the view that the benefit of securing individuals' commitment to retire at a given time—without any age-based requirement—is worth the expense.

Fair Exchange. Albino Barrera. *The Christian Century,* v. 121 pp22+ September 21, 2004.

When countries specialize in particular industries, Barrera argues, people around the world benefit. While the outsourcing of American jobs to other countries may have become a hotly debated topic in recent years, it is only one aspect of a larger economic trend that Barrera thinks will greatly benefit people in economically underdeveloped countries. While he acknowledges that the trend negatively affects some workers, Barrera points to India as one example of a country clearly enjoying the benefits of economic liberalization. Barrera cites biblical scripture to support his case.

Whose Tax Breaks? Ken Schroeder. *The Education Digest,* v. 68 pp72–3 March 2003.

Schroeder discusses a study from the National Education Association (NEA) that has found that local policymakers nationwide are allowing tax breaks and other subsidies to corporations with little or no accountability, frequently at public schools' direct expense, with school boards having no input in the decision. NEA president Reg Weaver notes that the group's study demonstrates that public schools are being shortchanged by elected officials who give away the store to corporations in the form of tax subsidies. He notes that these decisions, whether intended or not, hurt both schools and businesses in the long term.

How to Battle the Coming Brain Drain. Anne Fisher. *Fortune,* v. 151 pp121+ March 21, 2005.

Fisher points to a group of companies continuing to draw on their older workers in an effort to ensure that they are able pass their knowledge on to the next generation of workers. The methods used by these organizations could become a model for others, Fisher argues, especially the keeping of older workers employed for as long as possible, if only part-time, so that they can act as mentors for younger workers.

On Immigration Policy, We've Got It Backward. Geoffrey Colvin. *Fortune,* v. 152 p44 September 5, 2005.

Colvin argues that the U.S. should reform what he terms "our nutty immigration policy." Although the highly skilled workers who come to the United States on H1-B visas perform valuable work that Americans are unavailable to do and fill job vacancies, there is a restriction on the number of these visas issued. On the other hand, hundreds of thousands of illegal immigrants— many of whom evade taxes and some of whom take jobs from U.S. citizens by working for below-market wages—enter the country each year. The solution, writes Colvin, is to remove the cap on H1-B visas and encourage illegal immigrants to become tax-paying, on-the-books employees.

Is Your Boss Spying On You? Patrick Kiger. *Good Housekeeping*, v. 238 pp60+ January 2004.

Kiger writes that throughout the United States, growing numbers of employers are using high-tech gadgetry to monitor their employees in increasingly intrusive ways. In a 2001 American Management Association survey of over 1,600 firms, 82 percent said that they kept employees under some kind of surveillance—double the number of employers who admitted to doing this in 1997. As a result, the market for monitoring software is expected to rise from $140 million in 2001 to $2 billion by 2005, according to a study by AMR Research, a Boston technology research company. With a few exceptions, such spying is perfectly legal, and firms generally are not even required to inform employees that they are being scrutinized. Ways in which employers monitor their workers are outlined, and the steps that employees can take to watch their guard are discussed.

Beware the Interview Inquisition. William Poundstone. *Harvard Business Review*, pp18-19 May 2003.

In an article adapted from his book *How Would You Move Mount Fuji?*, Poundstone notes that companies have embraced high-pressure, puzzle-based interviews in the belief that candidates who can solve difficult questions under stress make better employees than those who cannot, but this is not necessarily the case. To Poundstone, puzzle interviews pose the same validation problem as intelligence tests: It is almost impossible to measure their efficacy because it is difficult to know whether candidates rejected by the employer for failing the tests would have made better employees. Nonetheless, puzzle interviews are probably no worse at spotting talent than conventional job interviews, which are notoriously bad at predicting future performance. According to Poundstone, more revealing is the situational or immersion interview, which thrusts candidates into scripted work situations, allowing employers to see how they handle the job. Tips are presented to help interviewers better evaluate candidates in the interview situation.

Masters of the Multicultural. Frans Johansson. *Harvard Business Review*, v.83 pp18–19 October 2005.

In a small number of forward-thinking firms, the diversity officer has taken on a new role, Johansson reports. Chief diversity officers flourished in the 1990s, as business responded to litigation and public pressure to show a more heterogeneous face. Now, however, some diversity officers supervise innovation efforts and generate revenues, Johansson contends. These people are likely to be more familiar with the cultural breadth and variety of their companies' talent than anyone else, and as a result they are in a great position to bring together different groups to produce innovation.

Alien Nation. Jennifer C. Berkshire. *The Nation*, v. 275 pp6–7 December 2, 2002.

Berkshire sees American policies and attitudes toward immigration as inconsistent: Immigrants are expected to perform tasks other Americans will not do for the wages offered, while at the same time the government prefers to keep as many immigrants as possible out of the country. As an example of this, Berkshire points to some 800,000 letters mailed to employers by the Social Security Administration that asked the companies to reconcile differences between the Social Security information provided and the Administration's records. According to Berkshire, the workers involved in these cases are very often immigrants, and this situation has led to perhaps 100,000 people losing their jobs.

A Spectacular Success? Eric Alterman. *The Nation*, v. 278 p10 February 2, 2004.

On the 10th anniversary of the NAFTA accord, Alterman reports, mainstream media accounts have expressed muted disappointment with its comparatively slight effects. A Carnegie Endowment study revealed that the accord did not come close to creating the amount of jobs it was expected to generate in Mexico. Instead, it devastated hundreds of thousands of Mexico's subsistence farmers and had little effect on jobs in the United States. At the same time, the expected advantages of the accord—that it would improve intra-American relations and reduce Mexican resentment toward their immense northern neighbor—have been more than offset by the costs of America's other actions.

Outsource, Outsource, and Outsource Some More. Daniel T. Griswold. *National Review*, v. 56 pp36–38 May 3, 2004.

An analysis of the information technology (IT) industry reveals that "foreign outsourcing" is just a buzzword for international trade in services, writes Griswold. Digitization of work through the personal computer and the high-speed and deregulated transmission of that information via broadband and the Internet mean that contracting for services abroad has become increasingly cost-effective. More and more IT companies are outsourcing such unappreciated jobs as routine programming, data entry, and system monitoring overseas. Foreign outsourcing means U.S. IT companies can dramatically reduce the cost of certain services, thus becoming more competitive in their core competencies and producing better and more affordable services for consumers and taxpayers.

Ignoring the Rich. William F. Buckley Jr. *National Review*, v. 58 p55 February 27, 2006.

Buckley discusses the political implications of news that a reduction in real income to the U.S. working class over the past five years has coincided with an increase in the share of national income going to the wealthiest 5 percent. The data provide ammunition to those who question the pretensions of the free market or want to heighten political means of interfering with its allocations. When a country is doing well, Buckley explains, the GDP is distributed mostly to people who do not need the money to live, but when these people invest the money, they do so to magnify its size. As a result, the capital is used to finance economic activity. The reduction in real average income by the lowest quintile of U.S. citizens has probably been caused by the lag between a rise in productivity and a rise in wages, writes Buckley, lags that are historically moderate and temporary.

Going South. Clay Risen. *New Republic*, v. 233 pp10–12 November 7, 2005.

Illegal immigration has become an important issue in the Southern United States, Risen says. For much of the 20th century, the South was defined by agriculture and low-wage, low-tech industries, but that started to change in the 1980s, as state governments attracted auto manufacturers and high-tech firms to the region and local companies such as Wal-Mart, WorldCom, SBC, and Wachovia made it onto the Fortune 500. In the mid-1990s, the rapidly modernizing Southern economy was facing a labor crisis, and Latino immigrants, legal and illegal, began filling the gap, settling in the suburbs where there were more jobs and housing. There has been a predictable backlash, Risen suggests, exacerbated by widespread social and employment insecurity among the region's newly expanded middle class, leading activists to stage rallies, distribute flyers, and organize anti-immigrant watchdog groups.

She Works, He Doesn't. Peg Tyre and Daniel McGinn. *Newsweek*, v. 141 pp44–52 May 12, 2003.

The writers report that many economists believe there is an increase in the number of American families in which the woman is the sole wage-earner. According to the Bureau of Labor Statistics, just 5.6 percent of married couples have a wife who works and a husband who does not, but many of the men who have put their careers on hold to watch the kids still have part-time or entrepreneurial work of some type, so they are not counted among that number. Analysis by University of Maryland demographer Suzanne Bianchi of new 2001 data suggests that 11 percent of marriages feature an Alpha Earner wife. White-collar men have been victimized by corporate downsizings, argue the writers, but many couples have merely decided it is not feasible to integrate two fast-track careers and kids without massive sacrifices. So they do a matter-of-fact calculation, measuring the size and upside potential of each parent's paycheck, and choosing to keep the bigger one.

Lifers. James Surowiecki. *The New Yorker*, v. 81 p29 January 16, 2006.

Job insecurity has become a regular source of worry for Americans, Surowiecki writes. A recent poll revealed that 46 percent of respondents feared that a household member would become unemployed in the near future, and that concern is a considerable factor in the current pessimism most Americans feel about the economy. Surowiecki contends that workers do have substantial grounds for worry, given that there have been significant changes in the types of risk that individuals have to bear, including the scaling back of benefits such as health coverage and pensions at corporations. Furthermore, the risk exposure of anyone who becomes unemployed has escalated.

What Is a Living Wage? Jon Gertner. *The New York Times Magazine*, pp38+ January 15, 2006.

The immediate aim for living-wage strategists, reports Gertner, is to put initiatives on the ballots in a number of swing states this year. An energetic grassroots campaign in Baltimore, led by a coalition of church organizations and labor unions, focused on the fact that many of the visitors entering homeless shelters and soup kitchens had full-time jobs. If the campaigners' reckoning is correct, the laws ought to bring about a financial gain for low-income workers and increase turnout for candidates who campaign for higher wages. Gertner writes that some members of the Democratic establishment have come to believe that the Left, after years of electoral frustration, has at last found its ultimate moral-values issue.

Deindustrialization. Roger Doyle. *Scientific American*, v. 286 p30 May 2002.

Doyle points to a novel theory about why manufacturing—and the type of relatively high-wage labor associated with it—continues to decline in the United States. Developing countries, with their comparatively cheap labor, have normally been considered the cause of the deindustrialization of more developed countries. However, according to a pair of international researchers, the process of economic development itself causes deindustrialization. These researchers contend that manufacturing naturally lends itself to standardization more than, for example, services do; productivity therefore increases more rapidly in manufacturing.

Cross Purposes. Jonathan Kandell. *Smithsonian*, v. 36 pp90–97 June 2005.

According to Kandell, as Mexican immigrants become more prosperous in the United States, they are transforming life on both sides of the border. By taking on menial work in the United States, Mexicans have not only raised their standard of living and that of their families but have also created a flow of capital back to villages across Mexico. That transfer of wealth—around $17 billion in 2004, double what it was only four years ago—has changed Mexican life, as new housing, medical clinics, and schools are being built. During this transformation, many of the assumptions, or even stereotypes, held in the United States concerning Mexican immigrants are being challenged.

Why Small Business Must Hire Offshore. *USA Today Magazine*, v. 133 p16 December 2004.

It is essential for small U.S. businesses to hire outside the country, the writer argues. John A. Challenger, CEO of the Chicago-based global outplacement firm Challenger, Gray & Christmas, Inc., argues that outsourcing is a matter of survival for small companies, particularly in the information technology sector, where payrolls can represent a company's highest costs. Challenger suggests that companies with fewer than 500 employees could argue that, because they are the top creator of jobs and are competing in the global marketplace, they should be exempted from a proposed law that aims to curb U.S. companies outsourcing jobs overseas.

Why Women Still Feel Persecuted. Judith R. Shapiro. *USA Today Magazine*, v. 134 pp22–24 January 2006.

For several decades, there has been tremendous energy and momentum toward the betterment of the lives of women, with sexual stereotypes that long existed as accepted wisdom being debated, deconstructed, and destroyed. Women are still a long way from equality in the workplace, however; there has not been significant expansion in the ranks of women as political office holders, for example, and the American record on this score is abysmal, Shapiro argues. The first step toward solving the problem of women's place in work and politics is admitting that a problem exists, and the second is agreeing that it is a serious and consequential one. There are gender-related differences in the ways in which women and men go about work and politics, but the questions should be asked more evenhandedly, and it should be clear which differences can be documented.

Why We Work. Andrew Curry. *U.S. News & World Report*, v. 134 pp49+ February 24, 2003.

As part of a special section in this issue on work, Curry discusses the history of work in America during the 20th century. In 1933, the Senate passed a bill that was narrowly defeated in the House that would have instituted a 30-hour week. Franklin Delano Roosevelt hit back with a new gospel of consumption that still thrives today. Work today dominates Americans' lives as never before, as workers add extra hours at a rate not seen since the Industrial Revolution. Technology has supplied increasing productivity and a higher standard of living, but instead of working less, Americans' hours have remained steady or risen. Furthermore, many more women work so that families can afford the accoutrements of suburbia, effectively choosing consumption over leisure.

Local Labor Pains. Silla Brush. *U.S. News & World Report*, v. 139 p26 October 24, 2005.

Brush writes that day-labor centers have become the focus of a national struggle to overhaul the U.S. immigration system. Once common only in heavily immigrant communities, day-labor sites have been built all across the United States as the illegal immigrant population, now estimated at more than 10 million, has increased dramatically. While the federal government struggles to cope with this problem, local authorities are being forced to find solutions. According to experts, Brush reports, these centers have, over the past five years, increasingly been seen as a way to bring at least a semblance of order to a chaotic situation.

Index